BrandLeaders

AN INSIGHT INTO BRITAIN'S COOLEST BRANDS 2002

Australia • Denmark • France • Germany • Holland • Ireland
Italy • Malaysia • Philippines • Spain • UAE • UK • USA
www.superbrands.org

EDITOR-IN-CHIEF Marcel Knobil

AUTHORS Rebecca Barnes, James Curtis, Helen Jones, Tony Newton, Mark Tungate

EDITOR Angela Pumphrey

EDITORIAL ASSISTANT Emma Selwyn

DESIGNER Verity Belcher

ART DIRECTOR Adam Selwyn

BRAND LIAISON DIRECTOR Annie Richardson

Special thanks to:
Bill Colegrave and Richard Thomas – Directors, **Mintel** for providing a considerable amount
of market research material and **Waymaker** for providing Mediadisk and PR support services.

Other publications from Superbrands in the UK:
Superbrands ISBN: 0-9528153-6-2
Business Superbrands ISBN: 0-9528153-8-9
eBrandLeaders ISBN: 0-9528153-7-0

For more information on the above publications or other Superbrands publications which focus on Australia,
Denmark, France, Germany, Holland, Ireland, Italy, Malaysia, the Philippines, Spain, UAE and the USA, please
email brands@superbrands.org or telephone 020 7267 8899.

To order Cool BrandLeaders please call 020 8829 3000

Published by Superbrands Ltd
64 West Yard, Camden Lock Place, London NW1 8AF

www.superbrands.org

Printed in Italy. ISBN: 0-9541532-0-0

The Superbrands organisation is the independent authority on branding. It promotes the discipline of branding and pays tribute to exceptional consumer, business and e-brands around the world.

The organisation grants Superbrand and BrandLeader status to brands considered to warrant that award by an independent council of marketing experts. Different councils for the different fields of branding and for different geographical regions ensure that only the most deserving of brands attain the Superbrands credential.

The Superbrands organisation promotes the discipline of branding to the wider community through a number of channels. The organisation has published a variety of highly respected books including Consumer Superbrands, Business Superbrands, and eBrandLeaders. These have been accepted as 'branding bibles' containing the elite of the brands within the category and providing readers with information about brand history, values, key achievements and future direction.

The Superbrands organisation also hosts the only tribute events dedicated to the branding industry. It is at these events that brands are celebrated and individual campaigns and companies are saluted for their endeavours. Superbrands regularly commissions research and publishes data on branding and the branding industry and runs the highly acclaimed Superbrands website; a valuable resource and insight into the world of branding. The organisation has become the first port of call for information and comment on branding issues for key media around the world.

Cool BrandLeaders is a new initiative from the Superbrands organisation. A dedicated Cool Council (listed below) has been formulated consisting of eminent individuals who are well qualified to judge which are the nation's coolest brands.

Through identifying these brands, and providing their case histories, the organisation hopes that people will gain a greater appreciation of the discipline of branding and a greater admiration for the brands themselves.

Beyond this cool branding bible, the organisation is responsible for a dedicated Cool BrandLeaders site (see www.superbrands.org); Cool BrandWeek; events about cool branding; and is constantly appearing on TV, radio and in newspapers commenting upon cool branding.

RALPH ARDILL
Marketing & Strategic Planning Director,
Imagination

DANIEL BARTON
Marketing & Communications Manager,
Diesel

CARL COX
DJ/Artist

YAN ELLIOTT
Copywriter, Mother

MARCEL KNOBIL
Chairperson, The Superbrands organisation

OWEN LEE & GARY ROBINSON
Creative Partners, Farm Communications

DERMOT O'LEARY
Presenter

RANKIN
Dazed & Confused

COSTANTINO SAMBUY
Marketing Manager, Piaggio

DANIEL SCHWALB
Marketing Director, Red Bull

ALON SHULMAN
Chairman, World Famous Group

DON SMITH
CEO, eyestorm.com

DARREN THOMAS
Managing Director, Cake Group

Cool brands you might think ride for a fall. Cool can all too quickly become the opposite of cool, as we seek out the latest and search for the most distinctive means of self-expression. Popularity, for which most brands strive, can destroy cool. The list of brands in Superbrands' Cool BrandLeaders however paints a different picture. Many have been around for decades and many more have achieved fame. British Brands Group, as the collective voice for brand manufacturers in the UK, is pleased to pay tribute to these brands that deliver the promise and demonstrate such acute understanding of their supporters.

JOHN NOBLE Director, British Brands Group

It is important to recognise the value of cool brand leaders. This Cool BrandLeaders book showcases over 50 excellent examples of popular and extremely desirable brands. To be a cool brand today has kudos and what about tomorrow? How does a brand remain contemporary? Cool brands need to do more to maintain relevance in a changing environment. Often the mark of a successful brand is how it is managed to maintain and broaden relevance over time. Those brands that go the extra mile and which adapt and respond to the changing needs of their customers will be winners. A brand that fails to adapt its offering will quickly become obsolete. Survival means change. And if a well-established brand can inject surprise and excitement then it renews itself. To succeed you need to know what makes your customers tick, involve them, stay close to them. No business is too big to recognise the customer is the pivotal figure. Essential to maintaining your cool at all times is challenging what a brand stands for to achieve sustainability and long term return on investment.

MIKE JOHNSTON International Chairman, The Chartered Institute of Marketing

As the trade body for the UK's advertising, media and marketing communications industry the IPA wholeheartedly endorses this latest branding book in the Superbrand series. This collection of 'supercool brands' is really good for our business – it lionises the great talent which built them, inspires other creative people to do likewise and reminds companies how valuable their brands can become when nurtured by the really talented professionals in the creative industries.

HAMISH PRINGLE Director General, Institute of Practitioners in Advertising (IPA)

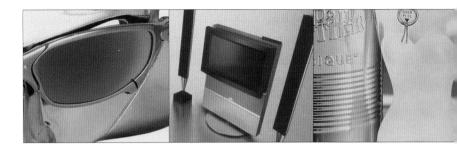

The Superbrands organisation is the independent authority on branding. It exists to promote the discipline of branding and pay tribute to exceptional brands. Never before though has it identified the nation's coolest brands. Perhaps, because this represents such a tough challenge.

The Superbrands Cool Council was formed to satisfy this challenge. It consists of a collection of individuals who have been responsible for creating numerous cool brands and whose views on this area are highly respected throughout the industry. They have selected an elite of brands (from an initial list of thousands) that qualify for Cool BrandLeader status. The following pages provide an insight into a number of them.

The criteria the Council referred to was: 'Cool BrandLeaders are brands that have become extremely desirable among many style leaders and influencers. They have a magic about them, signifying that users have an exceptional sense of taste and style.'

To state something is 'cool' is almost uncool. Yet, there still appears no better word to describe these brands that have come to own this magical yet indefinable quality.

A long while ago whilst I was at university I was invited to a friend's family party which was also attended by a millionaire. I remember my friend's grandfather whispering to me: "That fellow is a millionaire. Touch him and you'll also become one."

The Cool BrandLeaders book allows one to 'touch' many of the nation's coolest brands. It doesn't provide the formula for how to become one – no such formula exists. But it allows one to experience the history and development of these brands and to gain a precious insight into how they have been built. 'Sensing' these brands, and recognising the characteristics that appear to be ingrained in the majority of them, will help us become the pioneers of Cool BrandLeaders of the future.

Unfortunately, I never got to touch the millionaire.

MARCEL KNOBIL
Chairperson, Superbrands Cool Council
Founder, Superbrands organisation
Chairperson, Creative & Commercial

Knobil graduated from Manchester University in 1985 with a degree in theology. His thesis was entitled 'Ethical Issues in Advertising'. Since being awarded a postgraduate diploma in advertising in 1986, Knobil has worked at a number of agencies including as an account director at LansdownEuro (part of WPP, the world-leading communications group).

He now chairs Creative & Commercial. The company helps some of the strongest companies in the world (as well as emerging ones) create, build and enhance their brands.

Knobil constantly appears on TV and radio and is quoted in the national press on branding issues as well as lecturing on the subject throughout the world. This is Knobil's tenth book.

WHAT MAKES A BRAND COOL?
according to the Superbrands Cool Council

A cool brand:
colludes
challenges
knows who it's for (and who it's not for)
has a code
is collectable
has fans
has passion
is now
has folklore
feels close
is mine
provokes
makes me smile
doesn't try hard
A cool brand is....well.....cool.

RALPH ARDILL
Marketing & Strategic Planning Director
Imagination

A cool brand communicates its true personality with its consumer. It doesn't attach false values to the company or the products, as these are very transparent to our media and marketing literate audiences. It operates from within its target market and must genuinely understand and appreciate its customer's lifestyle and aspirations. It delivers on its promises at every point of contact with its customer whether it be quality of service, product or image. In most cases, a cool brand will naturally have an independent mentality (no matter how big the company gets) and never forgets its roots. But a brand is only as cool as its consumers, who are ultimately in charge of the brand image. Treat them well.

DANIEL BARTON
Marketing & Communications Manager
Diesel

I think that what makes a brand cool is something you have grown up with and is still around today ie. adidas, Puma, Levi's. I myself wear all of these items and I think these things that are very cool have stayed tested to time and as we lead into the 21st century the next generation are the ones that are going to carry on the coolness of these brands. I am looking forward to the new wave of cool wear that might take the place of some of these old school items, although, I am not sure if I will be around to see this but I am sure that this is what makes a brand cool.

CARL COX
DJ/Artist

Impossible to answer but there are certain things that need to be right to give you a chance of getting there. Make sure your product is of 'quality', which in turn provides integrity. That way people will find you and they are the ones that define a brand as 'cool' not the brand itself. If you do feel the need to advertise then talk to people not at them. And that is supposing what you are offering needs to be 'cool' in the first place.

YAN ELLIOTT
Copywriter
Mother

There is no set formula for developing a cool brand. The discipline of branding is not a science. Yes, there are certain guidelines that one needs to be familiar with – but creating potent brands goes way beyond abiding by rules. Cool brands are invariably the product of a fusion of vision, creativity and originality.

You can't simply deconstruct a cool brand to establish what has made it cool like you can pull apart an engine to appreciate how it functions. Stating what makes a brand cool is as much of a challenge as describing the taste of avocado or defining beauty. It is so difficult to explain yet you know it when you experience it. If we could define the 'what' that makes a brand cool the magic would evaporate.

MARCEL KNOBIL
Chairperson
Superbrands organisation

Cool brands don't care what other people think. They do their own thing and let people find them. They never ask, "Are we cool?" And they never say, "We are cool." Cool brands are brave. They can be arrogant and elitist but always desirable. They turn up in places you don't expect them. Cool brands always have a purpose beyond being cool. They set out to be the best in their field whether that be fashion or coffee machines. They don't need to think too hard about their brand essence, brand triangle or brand print. They are concentrated and don't take kindly to dilution. Cool brands are happy with who they are. They zig when others zag, but they'd never ever put it that way.

OWEN LEE &
GARY ROBINSON
Creative Partners
Farm Communications

For me, what makes a cool brand is almost a contradiction, because it should retain an air of exclusivity but at the same time, appear to be achievable for everyone. Wagamama do a great job at this, as their product and brand always has an air of the aspirational, but never at the expense of getting rid of the everyman feel. At the end of the day, a brand is useless if the standard of the product cannot back up the image.

DERMOT O'LEARY
Presenter

The thing is, it's no coincidence that the word 'cool' is so often preceded by the word 'effortless'. Truth be told, there is no other kind. If you have to try then you've already failed; if you want it too bad you're just chasing your tail. Because cool by it's very definition is not caring what anyone else thinks. It's dispassionate, free-willed, self-confident and non-impressionable.

The fact is cool is just a by-product. For some brands this is true, for others, it must at the very least appear so. Existing solely in the eye of the beholder: 'cool' is a quality bestowed upon those who don't seek it by those to whom it appears unobtainable, mysterious and seductive.

For a brand to appear cool in the same way that an effortlessly stylish friend appears cool takes the same process. By not trying to be cool, but concentrating instead on being honest, innovative, individual, interesting, amusing and original, cool will come along in it's own good time. The effort then can be justly spent on maintaining the illusion by staying focused and protecting it from exploitation, complacency and the pitfalls of believing in your own hype.

RANKIN
Dazed & Confused

A cool brand inspires passion, quickening your heartbeat and creating an emotional connection between you and an inanimate object. If you see a Mini Cooper being towed away it inspires emotions which just aren't there if it's a Ford Fiesta. You find yourself empathising with the car. It's a question of personality rather than the functionality of the product, an almost indefinable something which puts other brands in the shade. Our relationship with a cool brand is something very personal which we feel says something about us, so we want to share (or show off!) our allegiance. That's why cool brands are taken up by the younger generation who are usually more emotional, free spirited and have an unfettered personality and lifestyle. Cool brands will not appeal to – or be accessible by – everyone. They stand slightly apart, hence their coolness. How does a brand become cool? Timing and consistency. It has to be in the right place at the right time and maintain its personality without becoming stale.

COSTANTINO SAMBUY
Marketing Manager
Piaggio

Many people expect a 'how to built a cool brand guide for dummies' in articles like that. But the simple answer is it is not you, it is your consumer that makes the brand or product you are looking after, cool.

In today's consumer goods marketing a cool brand can be everything from a movie or a trainer to a website. What make them a cool brand is simple that they have a larger brand meaning than their competitors for their customers. Naturally these changes are through the overall mood in a society.

The key elements of a cool brand are; relevance to consumers; let consumer discover the brand initially for themselves; let the concept credibility spread via visual (opinion leader programs, viral (email) and verbal (word of mouth); if the brand becomes mainstream stay loyal with your core groups.

So maintaining a 'long-term sustainable coolness' is up to how able you are, to stay relevant to your consumer and engage with them.

DANIEL SCHWALB
Marketing Director
Red Bull

'Cool' has become an often used and much abused media watchword for defining and signalling the swings and roundabouts of cultural change, particularly in areas like music, fashion, consumerism, the media, food, drink and the arts. We've become so addicted and enslaved by dictates of cool that it has become a kind of new religion spawning its own industry.

Cool as we live and breathe it is impossible to categorise. And why do we need to? Everyone finds his or her own style, their own niche. Youth culture is all about style surfing. You can dip freely in and out of fashions, clubs, sounds and even decades to create the individual lifestyle that is right for you at any given moment. We create our own trends by amalgamating what we want from the countless genres of culture that are constantly being thrust at us by every medium and at every opportunity. If we like something we include it in our lives as easily as we reject what we feel to be unnecessary.

Today anything and everything has the potential to be cool – it is probably easier to be cool than to be uncool. So, in answer to the question, what makes a brand cool? I would have to say that it is the brand itself and the brand guardians who dictate the way in which the brand is perceived.

ALON SHULMAN
Chairman
World Famous Group

"If a man makes a better mousetrap than his neighbour, though he build his home in the woods, the world will make a beaten path to his door." (Source: Ralph Emerson) Brands start and finish with the product and if your product is cool your brand can be cool – people know it and you can't fool them. But it's not automatic and like every other part of business the brand must be worked and polished, and it can't be done by formulae. Imagination and excitement permeate every aspect of a cool product and by extension its brand, transforming expectations and expanding understanding of the product. Without change what is cool today will be cold tomorrow and without substance what is fake today will be failed tomorrow. Here are some more words from the 19th century for the 21st: "Preach not because you have to say something, but because you have something to say." (Source: Richard Whately, Bishop of Dublin 1850)

DON SMITH
CEO
eyestorm.com

The first lesson in chasing cool is don't – trying too hard becomes very obvious and turns off the very people you are trying to reach. Cool is about securing the perception that a brand is being true to itself and appearing natural. In order to stay true you have to start at the brand – unlock its essence and make that relevant to the target. This allows brands to have an attitude, an outlook, a way of doing things or a stance. This is key to attaining cool status; standing for something. Dare to be different, challenge the consumer to sit up and take notice, be clever, build emotional ties with the consumer, make them laugh, make them react but importantly do it with insight, with courage and with intuition. Inevitably cool brands can polarise opinion – by default they can't appeal to everyone but are usually appreciated by the majority. Confidence (to live with this) is thus vital for cool brands.

DARREN THOMAS
Managing Director
Cake Group

The heroism of world-class athletes is an inspiration to everyone. The brand that helps them reach the pinnacle of sporting achievement – adidas – is more than a pair of shoes or a running suit. It is a set of values, such as inspiration, invention, commitment and genuine experience. These transcend sport – they apply to life itself, with as much relevance to a kid in the city as an athlete on the winner's podium.

adidas's history dates back to 1920, when Adi Dassler, a Bavarian shoemaker, made his first pair of running shoes. Dassler's designs were quickly noticed and, at the 1928 Olympic Games in Amsterdam, Jesse Owens, sprinted his way to four gold medals in Dassler's spikes.

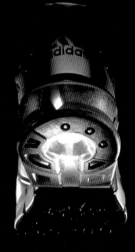

adidas has been part of many athletes' remarkable stories, from Muhammad Ali to Franz Beckenbauer and Illie Nastasse. It is no wonder that adidas has an iconic status few other brands share. Through its history, over 800 world records and medals have been won by athletes using adidas footwear and clothing at Olympic Games and World Championships. These are not mere statistics – each is a story of personal triumph.

It was not until 1948 that the adidas name and identity we know today was born. Dassler knew the importance of an easy to remember name and recognisable logo. He decided on 'adidas' – a word phonetically derived from his own name – and a logo consisting of three stripes that had initially been invented to provide more mid-foot stability in Adi Dassler's sport shoes.

This simple identity has become instantly recognisable throughout the world and is synonymous with sporting excellence and athletic endeavour. The genuine respect adidas has for sport is manifested in its obsession for making the best performance products for athletes. This is reflected in adidas's ability to get under the skin of sport.

A key element of the brand's DNA is its continuing position at the pinnacle of technological development within the sporting arena. At the forefront of this is the Forever Sport technology which umbrellas adidas's latest innovations. This includes the ClimaCool™ range of training shoes, which provide ventilation and breathability, as well as the a3 trainer (pronounced 'a cubed') with its revolutionary new heel technology.

As the adidas brand has matured, its values have resonated outside sport itself and spoken to contemporary culture. Since the early 1990s, adidas has transcended sport through to youth culture, capturing the imagination of young people on a global scale. Associating the brand with sports icons like David Beckham ensures that the brand is not only synonymous with excellence and success, but also with an individualistic style and attitude.

In addition to such associations, the brand's powerful and on occasion quirky advertising also enhances the brand's image. adidas uses a wide range of media – from giant 80-foot high billboards to the internet. Sponsorship and support of some of the world's top athletes and teams, as well as at grass roots level, has also helped adidas successfully position itself as the brand of choice in sport.

adidas still has Adi Dassler's genuine respect for sport, which is manifested in its obsession for making the best performance product for athletes on all levels.

adidas.com

Agent Provocateur

Joseph Corré and Serena Rees unveiled the first Agent Provocateur store in London's Soho in 1994, complete with saucy boudoir interior and glamorous assistants in uniforms designed by Vivienne Westwood. Over the past eight years, the glamorous, erotic designs, based on a concept of pure seduction, have been sold to women from all walks of life from schoolgirls to supermodels, rockstars to housewives, as well as transvestites and businessmen buying for their girlfriends, wives, mistresses, or indeed themselves.

With a refusal to follow fleeting trends, Agent Provocateur believes that an intimate relationship starts with the garment the customer selects and is fulfilled through the service they receive and the quality of the product they purchase. Agent Provocateur also maintains that the only thing more important than the way a garment looks is the way that it feels.

In 1995 the promotional ball was set rolling with the Agent Provocateur 'girl search'. Twelve finalists became infamous when they paraded outside London Fashion Week holding banners proclaiming, 'More S&M, less M&S!', a statement which proved ironic when Agent Provocateur later teamed up with the high-street chain to produce a mass market range.

Also that year, the brand partnered Erikson Beamon to launch Precieux, a glamorous range of jewellery with a fetishistic air, featuring handcuffs, whips and collars hand crafted using Swarovski crystal.

Corré and Rees have always had a unique approach to marketing, using shop windows (one of which even provoked one outraged passer by to call the police), catalogues and events which attract wide ranging national and

Colourful, glamorous and witty lingerie designed to arouse and amuse both wearers and their partners

international media coverage from the likes of Vogue, The Face, Elle Decoration, The Sunday Times and Playboy. Agent Provocateur's risqué cinema advertising featuring celebrities such as Kylie Minogue also makes a splash. Viewed by over 400,000 visitors to the website in January 2002 alone, the Kylie ad had men drooling everywhere.

Agent Provocateur was asked to join the prestigious Cutting Edge exhibition at the Victoria and Albert Museum in 1997 and a selection from the mail-order range was included in its permanent collection. The same year saw the opening of a second London shop in Knightsbridge, which was inspired by 18th century French high culture and featured Chinese motifs and a private changing room for discerning shoppers.

Another cultural accolade was scooped in 2000, when the company contributed to the Inside Out exhibition at London's Design Museum. The exhibition travelled the world until 2002, stopping off in Japan, Russia, Poland, Finland, Hong Kong and the Philippines. Also in 2000, the seductive Agent Provocateur Eau de Parfum was launched in the UK with a notorious party and provocative advertising campaign. Extentions to the perfume range starting with the AP Sauce Body were introduced the following year.

A-list celebrities were welcomed to the launch of the Agent Provocateur Los Angeles store in October 2001. The design was a veritable cocktail, mixing futuristic silver wallpaper with oversize neon tropical flowers and authentic English shop fittings. Meanwhile, the fragrance went on to win the 2001 FiFi award for Best New Fragrance and a specially created award for Creative Imagery. A busy year was rounded off with an invitation from the V&A's Textile and Dress department to design and fill two of its large museum displays.

Agent Provocateur has become a huge success, with brand extensions such as its hardback mail order catalogue, which was shot by leading photographer Tim Bret-Day. Led by its instinct for beauty and eroticism, Agent Provocateur remains committed to creativity and originality in maintaining the sexiness of the brand.

agentprovocateur.com

ALEXANDER
McQUEEN

Calm and collected Alexander McQueen is a superb craftsman who produces clothes that are at once dramatic yet commercial. Rather than relying on straightforward marketing techniques, his status is certified by the support given from his A-list clientele.

The breadth of the McQueen appeal was illustrated by the theatrical Paris catwalk show in March 2002 which was hailed as 'the most beautiful show of the season' by Italian Vogue. As well as creating influential clothes that directly inspire high street trends, McQueen has recently moved into designing eyewear. More store openings and a perfume launch are to follow, and it is clear that Alexander McQueen is on the cusp of becoming a global brand to be reckoned with.

McQueen was born in the East End of London in 1969, the son of a taxi driver and the youngest of six children and his rebellious genius became apparent when he spent most of his time at his all-boys school designing dresses for women. At sixteen he began carving out a stellar career in the unlikely world of fashion and walked straight into Anderson & Shepherd on Saville Row, determined to learn bespoke tailoring the traditional way. He moved on to Gieves & Hawks and the theatrical costumier Angels & Bermans, ultimately mastering six different styles of pattern cutting – from 16th century melodrama to sharp modern tailoring. Today, his clothes can embrace

Injecting a spirit of punk rebellion into high fashion

both extremes and he has been described as a better cutter than Yves St. Laurent.

By October 1996 McQueen had become chief designer at the French couture house Givenchy. With collections soon propelling him into the top slot, and his growing list of fans from the worlds of rock and cinema, he soon became a star in his own right. McQueen was named British Designer of the Year in 1996 and 1997, and again in 2001.

Since McQueen left Givenchy because, he argued, it was sapping his creativity, he has gone from strength-to-strength, creating wildly theatrical shows that have helped to re-establish London's status as a fashion capital. His clothes, blend drama and controversy with down-to-earth street style. While a recent show in Paris featured a woman dressed as a purple version of Little Red Riding Hood – complete with two wolves – most of the clothes were wearable as well as creative. And, of course, impeccably cut. Influential items included tweed, satin and leather skirt-suits, jackets with hoods and billowing sleeves, trousers with curved hems, and knitted tank-tops.

In previous collections, McQueen has enjoyed mixing the sinister with the romantic, and military and fairytale touches often appear side-by-side in his work, which he describes as being 'for the strong woman'. McQueen is launching a bespoke menswear range for Autumn/Winter 2002 in collaboration with H. Huntsman and Sons, the classic British Savile Row tailor. The eyewear collection is another new departure, and McQueen has also promised to launch a perfume in 2003.

There are currently two Alexander McQueen stores located in New York and Tokyo. Further stores in London, Milan and LA will be opened in 2003. This will no doubt ensure that he joins the list of designers who have ceased being mere names, and turned into bywords for style.

alexandermcqueen.com

In 1977 the Apple II put the company founded by school friends Steven Wozniak and Steven Jobs on the map. In the new personal computing market that was emerging, it was the biggest selling computer ever. As PC ownership soared with IBM imitations running Microsoft's Windows operating system, saturating the market, Apple began to focus on niche creative and scientific industries such as design, publishing and biotechnology. It quickly developed a legion of loyal fans and became renowned for being incredibly powerful whilst fun and intuitive. From there Apple's G3 processor made its computers the fastest of their kind, with the launch of the G4 processor breaking further speed boundaries.

Apple's first laptop computer, the PowerBook, was launched in 1991 for working on the move. Updated versions became ever slimmer and more powerful evolving into the Titanium PowerBook, which boasts a 15.2 inch wide screen. The iBook is in essence a scaled down PowerBook but is a more affordable range aimed at home and educational use.

Although Apple promoted itself for business and personal use, it was the former that it became best known for until the release of the iMac in 1998, which changed its key focus and the fortunes of the company. This revolutionary computer turned industry convention on its head and heralded a new direction for Apple, characterised in its advertising with images of world-changing individuals such as Albert Einstein coupled with the strap line, 'Think Different'.

Like absolutely nothing before it, the iMac was an all-in-one unit with the hard drive and monitor contained in a singular, curvy semi-transparent case. The removal of a floppy disk drive arguably signalled the end of floppy disks as useful media – if files fitted on one then they could be emailed. By far the most fundamental challenge to PC convention, however, was the styling – replacing standard grey and beige plastic with first turquoise, then 'fruity' colours such as grape and key lime. Homes, offices and classrooms across the world embraced the iMac's funky shape and colours, rapidly becoming a style icon and must-have fashion accessory. Subsequent releases have included psychedelic and Dalmatian patterns and are as likely to find their way into style bibles as any conventional fashion brand.

Apple has gained its edge through the way in which it continues to push technology that excites and exceeds expectations, generating anticipation even before people realise what it is capable of. The launch of the next generation, super sexy iMac was no exception and even challenged its own formula. The long awaited 15 inch flat panel iMac has a tiltable screen which appears to hover in the air above its base. This is also the first iMac to incorporate a G4 processor and 'SuperDrive' that can burn both CDs and DVDs.

Other key products in Apple's range include the ultra-fast silver G4 PowerMac and accompanying 22 inch digital flat-panel Apple Cinema Display. Apple's iPod is a portable MP3 player that can hold up to 1000 songs. AirPort is a wireless system that enables Mac users to surf the net, send and receive email, print and share files without the restriction of wires. Free software applications from Apple such as iTunes, iMovie and iPhoto let you organise and edit digital music, video and photos. Major third-party applications are also widely available for Macs. In 2001 Apple released its latest operating system, OSX, incorporating its groundbreaking 'Aqua' interface.

Apple has led the way in computing, software and hardware innovations for quarter of a century. Every system upgrade, industry shattering processor speed and must-have product extension affirms the real core of Apple's offering – coolness.

apple.com

Asahi
ASAHI BEER

Pure beer
Japan style

Super dry, super cool Asahi beer is the embodiment of modern Japan. Not the traditional Japan of tea ceremonies or picture postcards of snow-capped Mount Fuji but the Japan of the twenty first century — style, design and minimalism.

Asahi's clean, crisp, refreshing taste – 'Karakuchi' in Japanese – together with its funky metallic packaging and cutting edge advertising has ensured its rapid ascent. Asahi, which means 'rising sun', is the world's third biggest beer brand (Source: Impact 2000) and is available in 50 countries worldwide. Asahi was established

more than 100 years ago. Asahi Super Dry brand was introduced fifteen years ago. To ensure freshness for Asahi customers throughout Europe, Asahi has been brewed at the Branik Brewery, Prague, by Prazske Pivovary AS since January 2000. There, Asahi is brewed with identical ingredients and to the same exacting standards as in Japan.

Asahi is a distinctive, high quality alternative to mainstream European and American premium lagers. However, it is not a beer targeted at the mass market but is aimed at the cognoscenti – sophisticated, trend-setting consumers who are selective about what and where they drink. Careful decisions are therefore taken as to where Asahi is sold. It can only be found in cool bars, clubs, hotels and restaurants.

Asahi's advertising reinforces the brand's Japanese heritage with more than a hint of sarcasm. One campaign featured minor UK celebrities such as sports commentator Dicky Davies draped in a fur coat and singer Bonnie Langford playing golf. The accompanying text was a mixture of Japanese ideograms and stilted English translations such as 'remarkable and finesse so good'. The campaign was a sophisticated parody of Japanese advertising and its reliance upon celebrity endorsement. To many consumers, the kitsch campaign was confusing, but the target audience, the marketing literate, cool elite, got the point immediately and recognised that it was about understanding the unwritten rules of what is cool. Last year Asahi-branded cool rickshaws could also be seen carrying passengers through central London.

The latest campaign, which is again very stylised, uses a backdrop of white with a red circle, reminiscent of the Japanese flag. The line 'Pure beer Japan style' in each execution is accompanied with wise words on bar etiquette in a mock proverb style. The ads also feature young people high kicking or sitting in meditation positions.

Asahi also reaches young urbanites through sponsorship of selected projects. The brewery has produced guides to life in Tokyo and to the Japanese club scene, sponsored magazine inserts on Japanese food and drink, and published a guide to Japanese London in association with Time Out.

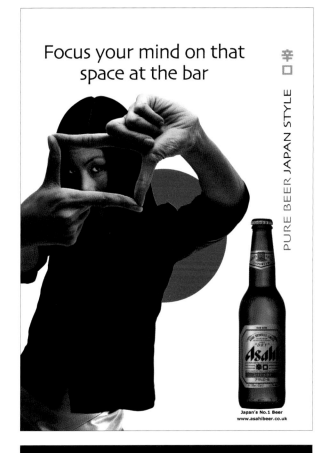

Asahi also supports art installations, cult films, fashion parties and music events as well as advertising in edgy, underground publications focusing on London's Hoxton art, music and fashion scene.

A joint promotion with Japanese retailer Muji and Asahi's support of Selfridges' month-long 'Tokyo Life' campaign which focused on Tokyo youth culture reinforced the aspects of Asahi's Japanese heritage which are in tune with western aspirations, expectations and values. This helped Asahi reach style conscious consumers fascinated by all things Japanese from its food and fashion to Manga comics and iMode superfast internet access via a mobile phone; from 'Kawaii' culture (a devotion to all things cute and fluffy) to high tech vending machines that dispense everything from noodles to CDs.

asahibeer.co.uk

AVEDA™

the art and science of pure flower and plant essences™

Committed to integrating balance,
wellness and beauty into daily lives

For more than two decades Aveda has worked to expand
the boundaries of beauty and business, developing products
made from plants and creating a company with a conscience.
Aveda, which means 'knowledge of nature', takes an ethical
approach to business. It supports the rights of indigenous
peoples and is also strongly against animal testing.

Plants are the starting point for virtually everything
Aveda does. Its research and development team is continually
seeking new uses for plant resources and more sophisticated
means of manufacture. It goes to great lengths to ensure
the authenticity, integrity and quality of its plant ingredients,
searching the globe for wild-harvested plants or those grown
without petrochemical fertilizers, insecticides, or herbicides.

This clear philosophy is based upon the principles of
Horst Rechelbacher, the founder of Aveda. From humble
beginnings in his Minneapolis kitchen, Horst has become a
world-renowned guru of well-being. To reach this pinnacle,
he has pursued the study of wellness, its origins in Eastern
and Western science and philosophy, and its relationship
to the essences and elements found in nature.

Horst is also a style leader in the hair care and the beauty
industry as well as a hair stylist, artist and entrepreneur.

He has drawn on his wide ranging expertise to direct the Aveda brand to encompass a total body approach — enhancing both internal and external well-being. Aveda products range from hair and skin care to aesthetics, makeup, massage and total body wellness. The brand also goes beyond just selling its products. Education is an important part of the brand's DNA and a global network of Aveda Institutes were founded to pass on Aveda's principles and knowledge. Under Horst's leadership, the Institutes have become internationally acclaimed centres of learning for professionals in cosmetology, hairdressing, manicuring, spa body care and massage.

In addition, Aveda Concept Schools have grown into a worldwide network of successful schools, educating students to become future leaders in the field of total body well-being. Aveda's Environmental Lifestyle Stores are a showcase for Aveda's flower and plant Pure-Fume™ aromas, skin care, hair care, makeup and lifestyle products — demonstrating Aveda's belief that businesses must utilise natural resources in a sustainable and responsible way.

Aveda do not advertise in the UK, but differentiate the Aveda brand through the concept of 'Aveda Experiences' which are complimentary in all of its stores. 'Aveda Experiences' are holistic services that can take up to ten minutes. They include Stress-Relieving Experience — a de-stressing massage, focusing on the scalp and back using balancing compositions and 'purescription' products; Hands-On Experience — consisting of a hand massage using Aveda aromas; Makeup Finishing Touch — a consultation with a professional makeup artist, designed to give a comprehensive lesson in the art of beauty; Sensory Journey — an experience which finds the best aromas and products to suit an individual.

Aveda's philosophy is also carried through to its head office in Minneapolis. Set in 65 acres surrounded by wetlands, most rooms receive direct sunlight via picture windows and skylights — even in the manufacturing and warehouse areas. During lunch, employees are free to take walks through the nearby wetlands, workout with a personal trainer in the corporate wellness centre or eat at Organica®, a natural foods restaurant that is also open to the public.

aveda.com

BANG & OLUFSEN

More than just technology,
Bang & Olufsen is about
innovation and intelligent
ideas that defy expectations

BeoLab 8000

We are blasé about radio these days, with more stations than you could name, tiny FM receivers and music blaring from speakers and earpieces all around us. So it's easy to forget that radio was once at the cutting edge of technology. People expressed doubts about the future of radio, just as later they were sceptical about the future of TV and, more recently, the internet. One newspaper wrote 'radio is a fashion trend, a phenomenon, which like spiritualism, jazz and embezzlement is a result of progress.'

That 'fashion trend' has stood the test of time pretty well. Along with it, Bang & Olufsen's reputation for quality has been forged, dating back to those earliest days in the 1920s when Danish entrepreneurs Peter Bang and Svend Olufsen created a radio with a natural sound. But they did something else too: they housed it in a walnut cabinet with maple inlay, transforming a quality radio from a merely utilitarian device into a piece of designer furniture. A status symbol that exuded style.

Although Bang & Olufsen has since diversified and now has a wide product range, everything the company produces remains based on the principle of combining state-of-the-art technology with innovative design. This has led to the inclusion of many thoughtful extra features such as glass doors that open at the approach of a hand or CD clampers that rise up to accept a disc and hold it in place while it spins.

BeoLab 2
www.bang-olufsen.com

BANG & OLUFSEN B&

Bang & Olufsen's range of TVs is strong from a technical standpoint, with features such as complete surround sound systems and a motorized stand that will turn to meet you when you switch the system on. This is combined with a range of options in terms of colours, screen sizes, formats and capabilities to suit a variety of tastes.

As the CD started to replace the LP, Asian competitors were producing stacks of hi-fi sets, anonymous black boxes which were almost indistinguishable from each other. Bang & Olufsen, with its emphasis on individuality, responded to the challenge by launching itself onto the CD market with a design classic: the upright, all in one Beosystem 2500.

Integrated systems which incorporate TV, DVD, VCR, radio and CD have also been developed, some with two motor-driven loudspeakers that stretch silently out to each side of the system. A step further on from this is BeoLink® which can operate equipment throughout the home and can even be used to control domestic lighting. Bang & Olufsen are also at the forefront of telephone technology, not only in terms of design but also by incorporating the latest ISDN technology into some models.

And last, but not least, Bang & Olufsen also has an ongoing vision to create the first truly invisible loudspeaker and to exploit the new world of sound that digital technology has opened up.

In parallel with attention-grabbing advances in technology and design, Bang & Olufsen has not neglected the need to reach its customers. The brand's stylish uncluttered advertising reflects the attitude of its style conscious consumers and also mirrors design elements used on the Bang & Olufsen website.

The brand has improved its distribution in the UK and can now boast a network of 50 stores, in addition to availability through independent shops and department stores.

bang-olufsen.com

BRITISH AIRWAYS

London eye

The Eye was conceived in 1994 on the kitchen table of London architects, David Marks and Julia Barfield. The husband and wife team designed the wheel as their entry for a competition to design a Millennium landmark for London. The project came to life two years later when British Airways offered to fund the project.

It took seven years and the expertise of hundreds of people from across Europe to then turn the dream into a reality. From the steel makers in Holland to the hub and spindle manufacturers in the Czech Republic, over 1,700 people worked on the project.

An observation wheel of this scale and sophistication had not been tried before and this created unique challenges for the team. In the Alps for example, an entire village tested the embarkation process on a mocked up boarding platform. On their journey through France to London, the convoy of lorries transporting the futuristic glass capsules had to take a special route to avoid certain bridges. Once all the components were in place over the River Thames, it took a week to lift the Eye into its vertical position.

At 135 metres, the London Eye is the world's tallest observation wheel and the UK's fourth tallest structure. Since opening in March 2000, it has had over eight million visitors, making it Britain's number one visitor attraction. It has won over 30 national and international architecture, design, tourism and people's choice awards.

The very best of British innovation, architecture, design and engineering

London giftwrapped

Treat someone to a special gift voucher, delivered anywhere in the UK and overseas.

0870 444 55 44

www.ba-londoneye.com

London eye

the view you can anticipate,
the experience you cannot imagine

BRITISH AIRWAYS
London eye

the way the world sees London

0870 5000 600
www.ba-londoneye.com

The Eye was always intended to be exclusive but not excluding and this is reflected in the visitor profile – everyone from week-old babies to those celebrating their 100th birthdays, from proposals to golden anniversaries, from S Club 7 to Archbishop Desmond Tutu. Fundamental to the design of the Eye and its facilities was the fact that it had to be accessible to all and, since opening, over 25,000 disabled visitors have flown the Eye.

Key to this success has been the careful positioning, design and management of the brand's truly unique offering. The logo embodies the Eye's visionary nature and supports its ambition of becoming an emblem for modern Britain. The circle is designed to represent 'a universal symbol of renewal, regeneration, harmony and hope'.

The London Eye also has thoughtful, stylish touches. For example, tickets and other communications referring to day time flights bear an image of the wheel by day; for evening flights, the wheel is shown by night.

In a very short space of time, the British Airways London Eye has become a symbol of modern Britain. Perhaps it is because of the constant, slow turn of the giant wheel and the unrivalled views it offers. Perhaps it is because it represents the steady march of time. Perhaps it is because it combines remarkable design and engineering to create an outstanding monument. Or, maybe, it is simply because it is so beautiful.

(cacharel)

PARIS

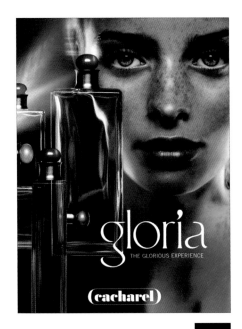

Recently relaunched with an upbeat new image and innovative design team, Cacharel ready-to-wear clothing enjoys a following on par with some of the largest French fashion labels. This enviable position is enhanced by the company's portfolio of fine fragrances, which have contributed significantly to the brand's recognition on a global scale.

Cacharel was founded in 1962 by the current President Director General, Jean Bousquet, who designed his very first pieces of clothing in Paris in the mid 1950s. The success of his creations prompted Jean to start up his own company, which he called Cacharel, a name inspired by a wild bird found in the marshes of Camargue in Southern France, an area with which Jean Bousquet has very strong links.

At the time, Cacharel was one of the first design houses to introduce the idea of ready-to-wear clothing as an alternative to couture designs. A young movie starlet of the time – Brigitte Bardot – wore brightly coloured Cacharel shirts tied under her bosom to launch the label.

Just a year after the company was founded, one of Jean Bousquet's shirts also appeared on the cover of Elle magazine. This exposure propelled the Cacharel label into stores worldwide and by the end of the year 300,000 shirts were sold.

In partnership with Annegret Beier, the creative force behind the packaging for all Cacharel fragrances, the first fragrance, Anaïs Anaïs, was launched in 1978. This classic, floral scent with its rounded bottle and delicately coloured packaging continues to be in the top five best-selling women's perfumes today in the UK, where 1.7 bottles are sold every minute.

Young, fresh and modern, Cacharel symbolises contemporary style at its best

The 1980s saw the creation of two more fragrances, Cacharel Pour Homme and LouLou, a sensual fragrance inspired by film star Louise Brooks. The following decade saw the introduction of three additional fragrances – Eden, LouLou Blue and Eau D'Eden. On the eve of the new millennium, NOA, the 'gifted fragrance' with its messages of wisdom and intuition, was born, winning the prestigious FiFi Award for Best European Perfume in 1999.

Gloria, the latest chapter in the Cacharel story of modern femininity, is poised to re-energise the fragrances portfolio with its colourful, sensual and dynamic 'rock chick' image and fiery romanticism.

In 2000, British husband and wife team Inacio Ribeiro and Suzanne Clements, known as Clements Ribeiro, took over the design and relaunch of the Cacharel ready-to-wear line. Long-standing fans of the Cacharel designs of the 1960s, they decided to tap into the brand's history for their first collection Spring/Summer 2001, indulging in a carnival of colour and pattern with a funky, modern twist.

The launch show saw Cacharel ready-to-wear returning to the Paris runways for the first time in twenty years, signalling a rebirth for the brand. One of the hottest tickets during Paris Fashion Week, the kudos of the brand was significantly elevated.

In early 2002, Clements Ribeiro designed a limited-edition bottle for Anaïs Anaïs. Featuring a beautiful, delicate pink signature toile de jouy print, the bottle celebrated in concrete terms the link between Cacharel fashion and fragrance. Cacharel now boasts over 1,000 retail outlets worldwide, including 55 stores. The Cacharel brand is embarking on a new and exciting journey for the 21st century. Rejuvenated, revitalised and more contemporary, the seeds for the future development of the Cacharel brand have been sown.

cacharel.com

COSMOPOLITAN

Celebrates fun, glamour and a passion for life, as well as inspiring women to be the very best they can

Three hours after it first went on sale in February 1972 Cosmopolitan magazine sold out. Its phenomenally successful UK launch followed an impressive US relaunch in 1965: the title had existed in the States since 1886 but was mainly devoted to fiction. At the time, Helen Gurley Brown, who founded Cosmo's re-launch and is now 80 years old, described prevailing attitudes to relationships and sex thus: "If you're single with no engagement ring in sight, then throw yourself off the Grand Canyon. If you're single and having sex, then it's time to stick your head in the oven."

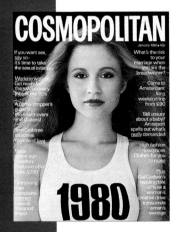

From the beginning, Cosmo spoke to women in a revolutionary way. For the first time sex and, more importantly sex-related problems, were discussed openly and frankly. Cosmopolitan has done as much, if not more, to educate women – and their partners – about sex and women's health than any other communication channel. In fact, The Times has described Cosmo as 'bigger than a magazine... a brand, an empire, a state of mind'. And despite having reached its 30th birthday, Cosmo has managed to retain its freshness, continuing to engage successive generations of women.

Cosmo is one of the flagship brands of the National Magazine Company, which claims to be the first publishing house to recognise the importance of magazines as brands. Its philosophy is to create and nurture brands, not just magazines, and to focus on developing and fostering readers' experience of the brand.

What makes Cosmopolitan different is its intelligent, upfront attitude and its willingness to boldly go where others fear to tread. It also manages to stay on the right side of the education vs. titillation divide. Cosmo knows that there are millions of young women out there looking for self-improvement, a rewarding job, a good relationship and better sex. The limits of what is considered 'decent' may have changed since the magazine's arrival on the UK scene, but the underlying desire to succeed, have great relationships and aspire to being the 'best you can be' remains. Young women still want to know what's 'normal', and Cosmo continues to reassure them that there is no such thing as normal.

As they say, imitation is the sincerest form of flattery – and one of Cosmopolitan's greatest accolades is the number of other publications that have tried to imitate its brave style, with varying degrees of success. None, however, lives up to the Cosmo style and there are now 47 international editions of Cosmopolitan, communicating with women all over the globe.

The Cosmopolitan brand has also diversified into other areas, such as licensed merchandise, carefully selected to fit with the brand's personality. Cosmo products include lingerie, hosiery, bags, swimwear, bedding, soft furnishings and eyewear ranges, plus an extensive collection of published books on sex, beauty and emotional well-being. There have been award winning Cosmopolitan Shows that attract a vast number of brands relevant to Cosmo readers under one roof combining a shopping experience and fashion shows with a variety of workshops from Cosmo experts.

There is also a Cosmopolitan café concept in the pipeline which will offer a range of express beauty treatments.

Cosmo's core business is magazines and it now has an extended family with Cosmopolitan Hair and Beauty and Cosmopolitan Bride. Recognising that girls are becoming young women at a seemingly ever earlier age, Cosmo launched CosmoGIRL! in 2000 aimed at 12-17 year old girls and matching its sister (or should that be mother) magazine in style and the belief that, whatever their age, Cosmo readers appreciate a brave and insightful standpoint.

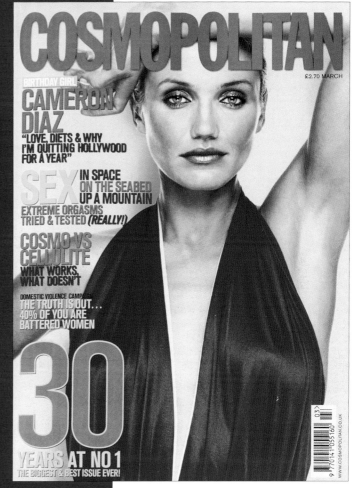

COSMOPOLITAN

£2.70 MARCH

BIRTHDAY GIRL
CAMERON DIAZ
"LOVE, DIETS & WHY I'M QUITTING HOLLYWOOD FOR A YEAR"

SEX IN SPACE
ON THE SEABED
UP A MOUNTAIN
EXTREME ORGASMS
TRIED & TESTED (REALLY!)

COSMO VS CELLULITE
WHAT WORKS, WHAT DOESN'T

DOMESTIC VIOLENCE CAMPAIGN
THE TRUTH IS OUT…
40% OF YOU ARE BATTERED WOMEN

30 YEARS AT NO 1
THE BIGGEST & BEST ISSUE EVER!

WWW.COSMOPOLITAN.CO.UK

cosmopolitan.co.uk

DAZED
&CONFUSED

Independent and irreverent;
radical and sexy

The style magazine, Dazed & Confused, co-founded by
Jefferson Hack and photographer Rankin, grew out of the
creative renaissance which gave London its cutting edge
reputation during the 1990s.

Then as now, it covers the most exciting, young,
independent, creative talent across fashion, music, film, art,
photography, design and literature — those people who bridge
the gap between the mainstream and the underground.
Dazed & Confused was launched as a reaction against
traditional media and other sanitised style magazines.

Pushing new ideas and ways of seeing things through
the best writing, reportage, design and photography, Dazed
eschews PR led product to set the agenda by starting trends
rather than following them. It doesn't believe in telling people
what to do, what to wear or what to be — it recognises that
its readers want to think for themselves.

As such, Dazed & Confused has attracted an extended
family of dynamic creative contributors and collaborators
which includes musicians Björk and Massive Attack, the fashion
designer Alexander McQueen and artists Sam Taylor Wood,
and Jake and Dinos Chapman.

Ten years on from its launch, Dazed & Confused is an
international phenomenon and is sold in over 40 countries
worldwide. It has won numerous awards including Front Cover
of the Year and Best Use of Photography in the Magazine
Design Awards, and this year was nominated for International
Magazine of the Year by the Periodical Publishers Association.

Dazed & Confused continues to accurately identify and
influence fashion aesthetics and cultural trends through both
its editorial and its design. It is an inspiration as much as
a commentator on global creative trends.

It is in this spirit that Dazed & Confused continues to set the agenda from directional and risk-taking fashion to editorial campaigns. It has supported initiatives such as Stop Esso and Jubilee 2000 through events and editorial as well as featured controversial fashion pages such as its bold Disabled shoot and depiction of models giving blood to raise awareness for the National Blood Association.

Still completely independent in ownership and spirit, the Dazed publishing group enjoys steady growth in revenue and circulation in a declining magazine market. The brand has diversified into other areas, exporting the Dazed & Confused style and attitude across media partnerships, both creative and commercial, to include live events, tours, exhibitions, supplements and books. Dazed has also expanded into film and TV production, launched the Vision On book publishing company, and opened a gallery. A wide range of projects are currently in production across different media including film, TV, online, CD Rom and DVD.

Underpinning the editorial and creative ethos of Dazed & Confused has always been the belief in showcasing and supporting new creative talent. This was strengthened last year with the introduction of an annual awards programme. Working with course leaders as well as established names from the fields of Fashion, Photography, Music and Graphic Design the competition aims to give young creatives the opportunity they need to succeed in an increasingly tough environment.

Now ten years old, Dazed & Confused has evolved into the 21st century without losing touch with its original risk-taking and independent ideals. This spirit will be consolidated and celebrated in its ten year anniversary at the end of 2002. This will be marked by a special birthday issue of the magazine drawing upon some of the established names that Dazed has worked with over the past decade, incorporating original commissions and collaborations from these personalities, creatives and celebrity faces. True to tradition, the anniversary issue and celebrations will continue to set this alongside the new, breaking names of the future.

confused.co.uk

DENIM

A striking backdrop for lounging about, looking good and pretending you're loaded

There was a time when going for a drink in London meant either standing in the corner of a packed pub, sitting in a wine bar with a bunch of braying yuppies, or becoming a member of a pricey Soho club.

All that changed in the mid 1990s, when a bunch of young Londoners got back from New York with the realisation that it was possible to create spaces that combine top-flight service, forward-thinking cocktail menus, and eyebrow-raising design. All of which has made London one of the best places in the world to down a vodka Martini.

The trend found its apotheosis in Denim, which has nothing to do with jeans but everything to do with studied cool. Richard and Antony Traviss opened the bar in 1998 and have since gone on to buy and remodel the achingly hip nightspot Brown's.

Both in their early 30s, the Traviss brothers are a world away from the public school educated sons of actresses and politicians who are often found at the helm of other such establishments. The pair were born in the East End of London to Maltese/Italian parents and did not have a privileged upbringing. Richard left school at fifteen, and his brother at sixteen. The pair have remained friends, despite their seemingly contradictory personalities – Richard is said to be extrovert and impulsive, while Antony is calm and meditative – and their mixture of determination and creativity has clearly paid off.

Denim itself is a triumph of ambition over realism. Now on three floors, with space available for hire, the bar in Upper St. Martin's Lane retains the highly colourful and futuristic ambience of the original, smaller venue. Antony – who spent time in the Far East – made sure the decor adhered to feng shui principles but there's more to it than the occasional carefully placed fish tank. The ground floor is lit by glowing pink screens and a huge mirror. The basement bar is adorned with throbbing red – to match the pulsating music, provided by superstar DJs who pull in their loyal followers. The final jewel in Denim's crown is an intimate mezzanine terrace restaurant. The food is as directional as the rest and is best described as a 'global fusion' of styles.

But the drinks are really the thing, ranging from champagne and imported beers to frothy-but-lethal concoctions like its vodka, blueberry and cream cocktail. With cocktails once again the preserve of the beautiful people, Denim's deluxe creations carry a price tag to match.

The bar has become a success with relatively little marketing, relying on its groundbreaking design to win favourable reviews and word of mouth recommendations. Considering it has been open for nearly five years now, Denim seems to have escaped the 'that was then' effect that has spelt the death of many a style-leading bar. Indeed, it seems on the verge of tipping into the 'classic' category. How long will it be before we see Denims springing up in Paris, New York or Tokyo? That's down to the brothers.

denim-lifestyle.co.uk

DIESEL®
FOR SUCCESSFUL LIVING

Diesel is a state of mind: it means being open to new things, listening to one's intuition and being honest with oneself

Diesel: jeans, casual clothing, accessories. Or Diesel: for successful living. Which really reflects the meaning of Diesel? Both?

From its beginnings in the Genius Group in Italy, Diesel had a strong message to convey. It has always been, in its own words, quirky, paradoxical, extravagant and nonsensical. (A quick look at the website confirms that.) It has also always been about fine design and quality clothing (and a visit to any of its 75 individually designed stores worldwide, will confirm that).

When Renzo Rosso founded Diesel back in 1978, he wanted the company to be a leader that took chances and occupied a distinctive niche in people's minds. He didn't want to just produce jeans, however well-designed and well-made.

So the design team turned their backs on the style-dictators and fashion forecasters. Famous for their eccentric self-planned research trips, Diesel's innovators now create clothing varied and unique enough to allow style-leaders around the world to wear Diesel whilst maintaining their own individual style.

Diesel adverts are elevated to the status of art – and present Diesel's personality so as to allow individual interpretation of their meaning. Style gurus have described them as 'the most original sustained campaign ever'. The 'For Successful Living' tag line (a dig at companies that promise lifestyles if you buy their products) shows Diesel at its ironic best and has become synonymous with the brand. The Diesel website contains an archive of its much-loved (and, incidentally, award-winning) advertising campaigns right back to 1990. The same irreverence pervades the Diesel catalogues. Far from being mere product showcases, each edition takes a radical new look at traditional graphic and photographic techniques. In effect, they too belong to the 'Diesel space'.

And that space isn't static but is always on the edge, always being extended. The main Diesel denim collection is full of unique details

and new washes and treatments. While other brands often focus on uniformity and a singular 'look', many Diesel garments are hand finished, making each one unique. More experimental and pioneering designs find a home in DieselStyleLab, a separate collection in its own right. There's also Diesel Kids: gutsy clothing for a gutsy generation that enjoys the same design ethic as its mother brand. And 55DSL, a strong and independent streetwear collection featuring anti-gravity clothing for lovers of intense action.

There's more, too. Time frames, footwear, spare parts, shades, underwear, even fragrances – all 100% Diesel in ethos, design and spirit.

The famous Pelican Hotel in Miami's South Beach district perfectly expresses the Diesel vibe. A haven of eccentricity, all rooms have been designed and decorated by Diesel's creative team as surreal movie sets. There's the 'Psychedelic(ate) Girl', a mind-trip from the past furnished with plastic furniture and posters from the 1970s ... or 'Me Tarzan, You Vain', a triumph of zebra stripes furnished in old safari style ...

or even ... 'Best Whorehouse' or 'Halfway to Hollywood'...

Also key to Diesel's success is its support of the idea that the young should be given the freedom to express themselves. This manifests itself time and time again through its support of up and coming creatives in the fields of music, fashion, art, film and new media.

Diesel has succeeded because it recognises its consumers' need to remain individuals. Because it doesn't take itself too seriously. And because the Diesel ethos is part and parcel of the personality of those that run the company. As Renzo Rosso says: 'Diesel is not my company; it's my life.'

DKNY

Since its launch in 1989, the fashion label DKNY has come to represent the energy and spirit of New York. Like the Big Apple, DKNY is international, eclectic and fun. Embracing real life and all its personalities, DKNY was created as the street-wise counterpart to Donna Karan New York, a luxe Collection known for its cashmere and hand-painted devore dresses. As Karan herself says, DKNY is "The pizza to Collection's caviar." She called her new brand DKNY, inspired by the sound and rhythm of FDNY and NYPD, shorthand for New York City's fire and police departments.

From the start, DKNY has always been about fast fashion with an urban mindset. Having previously broken new ground with Donna Karan New York, the designer wanted to dress her other, more casual lifestyle, while keeping a sophisticated edge. "I wanted jeans that would fit and flatter a woman's body," she explains. "Everything out there was designed for boy-like figures and from a very young point of view. I envisioned a collection designed like a real wardrobe, with flexible, interchangeable pieces polished enough to wear one way to work and hip enough to wear another way on the weekend." At the time, such a collection didn't exist. DKNY trail-blazed a new category, called 'bridge' in the fashion industry, that lived between designer and inexpensive sportswear.

DKNY has something for every age, mood and lifestyle; from tailored suits and vintage-inspired dresses, to leather motorcycle jackets and jeans, to yoga-wear and spirited evening wear

A brand inspired and energized by its New York City roots

dkny.com

perfect for clubbing. "DKNY is one-stop shopping," says Karan. "It's all here under one roof, from the classic and timeless to the super trendy and of the moment." DKNY grew so popular and diverse that it gave birth to a family of companies, such as DKNY Men, DKNY Jeans, DKNY City, DKNY Active, DKNY Kids, DKNY Underwear, as well as DKNY Eyewear and DKNY Shoes. There are also myriad DKNY accessories lines to complement every season, including handbags. Everything has an unmistakable New York sensibility.

Over the years, DKNY has come to represent not only an attitude, but also a lifestyle. DKNY fragrances for men and women were introduced and quickly became best sellers. A multifaceted home furnishings collection called DKNY Life, created to dress the urban home in fashion textures and innovative accessories, was also launched. DKNY is so tied to New York City, that its advertising often features Manhattan as a backdrop.

DKNY has exploded out of New York, becoming one of the city's most famous exports. There are now over 70 company owned or licensed DKNY stores worldwide. Since DKNY is as much uptown as it is downtown, there are now two flagship stores in New York City – one on Madison Avenue and 60th Street, the other on West Broadway in SoHo. Both are the spiritual homes of the brand, bringing DKNY back to where it all began.

DUCATI

A legend built on racing and passion

Ducati motorcycles are the most coveted in the world, due to the brand's racetrack heritage, Italian design, state-of-the-art engineering and victories in the World Superbike Championship. The Ducati range now includes four families: Superbike, Supersport, Monster and SportTouring.

The Ducati family founded a company in 1926 making radio components with other Bolognese investors. By the 1940s they commanded a global business from a sprawling factory complex, which was destroyed during World War II. But Ducati rose from the ashes in a different guise, making small auxiliary motors for bicycles, then motorcycles. When pioneering engineer Fabio Taglioni arrived in 1954, the company moved into high gear. A highlight of this period was the introduction of the 'desmo' valve gear – which has been a feature of Ducati bikes ever since.

The 1980s and early 1990s saw Ducati reach new heights launching the legendary Ducati Monster, and the luscious Supermono.

In 1994 one of the most significant motorcycles in Ducati's history was created – the 916. Winning numerous awards not only in motorcycling and also the design and art world too, the 916 is a timeless classic. The 916 evolved into the 996 and now 998 and soon proved its racing pedigree by winning numerous national Superbike Championships around the world. Nine World Superbike riders titles and ten Constructors titles mean Ducati is the most successful manufacturer ever.

In the late 1990s Ducati launched the Monster Dark, which became the best-selling motorcycle in Italy. Ducati then began to expand into accessories and clothing. The creation of stand alone Ducati stores then commenced.

Through advertising and public relations, the company has created a sense of community among fans and owners of the bikes – a group they labelled 'the Ducatisti'. This was underlined in 1998 with the first World Ducati Weekend, held in Italy. This event has since grown and the third event took place in June 2002. The Ducati website has also been developed to aid 'the Ducatisti' to keep in touch, as well as to attract new followers.

In 1998 the Ducati Desmo Owners Club was created. Run from Bologna, the club is an umbrella organisation for independent Ducati clubs around the world, allowing enthusiasts an opportunity to communicate with other Ducatisti.

Another mark of the brand's success came in 1999 when the company was listed on the New York and Milan stock exchanges.

Movie directors clamour to put the machines in their films, hoping that the bikes' savage elegance will rub off on their stars. Recently Wesley Snipes rode an ST2 in Blade II and Rebecca Romijn-Stamos rode a red Ducati Monster in the bone-crunching motorbike duel flick Rollerball.

Keen to get involved with co-marketing activities, Ducati launched a clothing range with DKNY which saw the brand name appear in distinguished fashion stores around the world. As well as clothing co-marketing, Ducati have also had associations with MAC cosmetics, Harrods and Roberto Cavalli.

"Every Ducati I own has a name and I kiss each one before and after every race."

DUCATI

Ducati People. Michael Tardio, 34, Restaurant Manager, USA.
Ducati 998R: new Testastretta engine, 999 cc, 104 mm bore, 139 HP, Öhlins fork and rear shock absorber
Ducati Performance Apparel and Accessories: 'Ducati Corse' suit,
Evolution boots, Superbike helmet, at Ducati Dealers and Stores.

ducati.com

Ducati is forward thinking in terms of product design and marketing. In 2000, the MH900e became the first motorcycle to be reserved by customers exclusively over the internet.

Ducati's community approach culminated in the launch of a new print advertising campaign, developing the brands 'Ducati People' theme. Via its website, the company encouraged owners of Ducati's to submit photographs of themselves and descriptions of their lifestyles. Out of thousands of submissions, Ducati picked 26 owners to be flown to Bologna and professionally photographed. The portraits show some seriously cool people, on some of Ducati's most awesome machines.

GAGGIA®

In the past, café culture was only associated with the European way of life. Now, however, this way of socialising and relaxing has become popular throughout the world and Gaggia are helping to fuel this trend.

Over 60 years ago Achille Gaggia's passion for making the ideal espresso led him to the novel idea of forcing hot water over coffee grounds rather than steam. Such was the success of this system, that machines bearing his name have taken the idea to cafés and restaurants around the globe.

A crucial step in the brand's evolution was the introduction of the Baby Gaggia in 1977. This was Gaggia's first domestic machine, and it capitalised on the surge in popularity of espresso coffee in the 1970s. For the first time, professional quality espresso coffee could migrate from the coffee shop to the home.

Gaggia's values of quality, reliability and style have always been central to the brand and have aided its position as a leading brand in the espresso machines market in the UK and Ireland, both in the trade and consumer markets.

Gaggia machines combine advanced, cutting edge technology with classic form, underscored by durability and elegance. In addition, Gaggia use materials that are both hardwearing and eye-catching. For example, the 'Classic' model uses carbon steel, black chromium plating and 24 carat real gold plating (or a nickel plating) as well as brass components which can maintain liquid at a constant temperature.

Gaggia takes the skill of being an expert coffee maker, or 'Barista', seriously and runs day-long Barista training courses, officially awarding Gaggia Barista Training Certificates to those who reach perfection.

Gaggia also knows that coffee lovers are individualists and has tailored it range to meet the variety of needs. Some coffee connoisseurs want perfect coffee from bean to cup at the touch of single button: others crave the ritual

of grinding beans and preparing the filter holder. Some want smooth curves and modern digital design; others prefer a retro-styled, lever operated model. Gaggia has models to meet the functional and stylistic needs of both commercial and domestic users. Where Gaggia really scores is in turning the perfect espresso into a matter of style as much as substance. Making the '50 Best Kitchen Appliances' list in The Independent is an indicator of performance, but getting into the '100 Best Things in the World' list in a title like GQ reflects both Gaggia's style and quality. As GQ put it, 'the Gaggia Syncrony Digital is perfect for those 'back to mine for coffee' moments…and the coffee isn't a euphemism.'

Lifestyle is an important element of Gaggia's design thinking. Its rolling development programme introduces new machines to adapt to new lifestyle concepts and bring new users to the Gaggia brand. It has also diversified into coffee grinders and the Gaggia Gelateria ice cream maker, which Delia Smith has used in her TV shows. However, the key to Gaggia's success is the style and attention to details which is carried through every Gaggia piece of equipment.

Goldsmiths
UNIVERSITY OF LONDON

The incubator of new British art

Based in South East London, creative and cosmopolitan, Goldsmiths College has a reputation as a hothouse for contemporary artists and is regarded by many as the most innovative university for the arts in Europe.

Since its foundation over a century ago in 1891, Goldsmiths has been a key centre for art and design education in Britain. For more than a generation it has defined worldwide artistic movements and nurtured some of the best known talents – from Mary Quant and Bridget Riley to Antony Gormley and Damien Hirst. In the last ten years, no fewer than five former students have won the coveted Turner Prize and almost a quarter of those shortlisted for the award since it began have been Goldsmiths graduates. The prestigious Beck's Futures award has shortlisted no fewer than seven past students over its three year span.

As a major Sunday newspaper wrote, Goldsmiths graduates "go on to paint, perform, design, and influence the way we think". Tate Modern and other contemporary galleries are awash with the work of Goldsmiths alumni who are often credited with starting the Young British Artists 'YBA' movement.

Goldsmiths' distinguished roll-call of alumni embraces many well-known figures in both the arts and public life including one Law Lord, two Cabinet Ministers, and a number of well-known actors, musicians, designers, writers and academics. More specifically, in the world of art and design, alumni include Grenville Davey, Lucian Freud, Antony Gormley, Damien Hirst, Mary Quant, Bridget Riley, Julian Opie, Mark Wallinger, Sam Taylor-Wood and Gillian Wearing. In the musical arena, Goldsmiths boasts alumni such as Graham Coxon and Alex James, John Cale and Malcolm McLaren. In the political arena, Lord Merlyn-Rees and Tessa Jowell. In media and entertainment, writers and journalists, Colin Welland, Molly Parkin, Corrie Corfield and Carol Sarler, entertainer, Julian Clary and the actors George Baker and Gwyneth Powell.

Goldsmiths – with over 8,300 full-time students, many from overseas, and another 4,000 on short courses – is one of the 'big eight' colleges of the University of London. Its mission is to be pre-eminent in the study and practice of creative, cognitive, cultural and social processes.

One of the keys to Goldsmiths' coolness is the liberal and creative approach to the teaching of all subjects – not just the arts – pioneered at the college. Another is that teaching takes place in a wide-ranging cultural and intellectual context. This creative approach extends into all areas of study and across all departments including the Centre for Cultural Studies, the Centre for Urban and Community Research, Educational Studies, Computing, Humanities, Languages, and Behavioural and Social Sciences.

This approach will soon be extended through the development of a unique, new Centre for Cognition, Computation and Culture. Rather than segregating departmental research, the Centre will provide advanced facilities to allow linked research in the areas of Psychology, Computing Sciences, Anthropology, Sociology, and Media and Communications.

In the words of the New Yorker magazine, Goldsmiths is 'the incubator of new British art', at a time when Britain leads contemporary art throughout the world.

goldsmiths.ac.uk

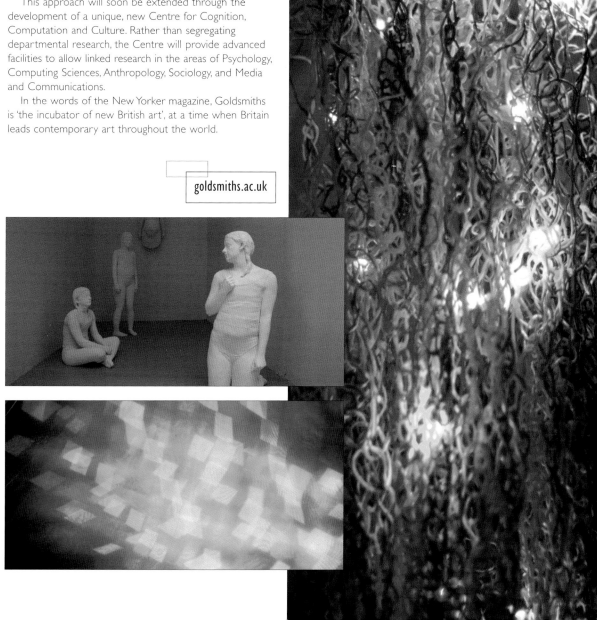

An intense experience of pure pleasure

Häagen-Dazs sparked a revolution in the 1980s when this previously unheard of brand took the ice cream market by storm and transformed a traditional kids dessert into a strictly adult indulgence – suddenly ice cream was sexy.

In 1988, Häagen-Dazs hit the UK market creating a niche for luxury adult ice cream which had never before existed. The brand was launched slowly and stealthily with distribution in upmarket stores such as Harrods, supplemented by sampling at celebrity parties and film premieres generating a 'whisper campaign' among stylish consumers.

The success of Häagen-Dazs was owed to a product which truly lived up to the brand ethos, made with the highest quality natural ingredients – fresh cream, milk, sugar and eggs with no artificial flavours or colourings. The rich and creamy density of Häagen-Dazs is created by maintaining an extremely high ratio of ice cream to air, unlike cheaper brands in which substantial quantities of air are pumped into the product. This essential component is evident when holding a tub of Häagen-Dazs and comparing this against another brand of ice cream. The tub of Häagen-Dazs will weigh much heavier.

In 1991 a £30 million European marketing campaign called 'Dedicated to Pleasure' brought Häagen-Dazs to the masses, creating a stir by

Sensual Eating

www.pathtojoy.org

featuring risqué pictures of young couples in intimate embraces. Provocative advertising focusing on semi-clad couples covering each other in ice cream appeared on TV and the big screen.

To further enhance and create a whole brand 'experience', the Häagen-Dazs Café was opened in premium locations around the world. In London's Leicester Square, the Häagen-Dazs Café replicates the brand essence with sumptuous sofas and cosy booths to create intimate cocoons, whilst also allowing customers to experiment with different flavours in a scooping area.

But as Häagen-Dazs radically changed the ice cream market, competition – from niche suppliers and supermarket own labels – began to emerge. To keep one step ahead of its rivals, innovative new flavours which reflect local tastes have been introduced. In Japan for example, Green Tea ice cream is a best seller, whilst in the UK, Häagen-Dazs recently launched Lemon Cheesecake, Tiramisu and Banoffee flavours to reflect the British taste.

In order to maintain its position as market leader, Häagen-Dazs has insured its advertising has moved with the times. 1998 saw a light-hearted take on the idea of perfection with the '100% Perfect' campaign. Memorable moments such as the old man with a beautiful young wife, unable to remember where he lives were served up with the message that 'at least Häagen-Dazs is 100% perfect'.

In 2001 Häagen-Dazs recognised sex was being used to sell everything from cars to soft drinks and thus moved on from its intimate stance of the 1980s choosing instead to emphasise the quality of the product as a pleasure giving indulgence. The latest advertising campaign called 'Path to Joy' takes a tongue-in-cheek look at new age spirituality – a spoof self-help group whose members expound the ultimate pleasures of Häagen-Dazs.

Häagen-Dazs remains the leading super premium ice cream on the market having established itself as a genuinely intense experience of pure pleasure.

haagen-dazs.co.uk

Hello Kitty®

A small white cat, with no mouth and a red bow. Just another kids' character, or a global fashion icon? Considering that this cute feline, Hello Kitty, has been driving girls of all ages mad for 27 years and sold $1.2 billion of merchandise in 2001, the brand certainly has icon credentials.

Sanrio, the Japanese gifts and accessories company, is the driving force behind the Hello Kitty phenomenon. The story began in 1974, when Sanrio launched a small purse featuring the simply drawn face of a cat, with thick black whiskers, button eyes and a curiously absent mouth. When demand for the purses soared, Sanrio began using the image on other products, such as stationery and small gift items. Kids loved them, particularly 8-12 year-old 'tween' girls, who remain Hello Kitty's most loyal fan base.

Now, young girls, teenagers and even grown women all over the world can't get enough of Hello Kitty. Sanrio places her image on a wide but carefully chosen range of products and accessories – from nailpolish and necklaces to boomboxes and toasters. In Japan, it's even possible to have a Hello Kitty wedding.

Hundreds of Sanrio boutiques around the world sell Hello Kitty merchandise, including flagship stores in famous neighbourhoods such as Tokyo's Ginza District and New York's Times Square. The key to Sanrio's success has been to respond quickly to fashion trends and popular culture, creating cool products which hit the spot every time. Initially, it was just little girls who lapped up the candy-coloured, fun-sized accessories but, as they grew up, the same girls kept buying Hello Kitty products, encouraging Sanrio to target older age groups, creating a true cross-generational brand in the process.

Adored by girls of all ages around the world

© 1976, 2002 Sanrio Co., Ltd

As a result, Hello Kitty remains a powerful kids' brand as well as a pop icon for older consumers. You're now as likely to see a nine year-old girl with a Hello Kitty pencil case, as a 25 year-old clubber wearing a Hello Kitty t-shirt. New products are reviewed in kids and teen magazines, but also in style bibles like Vogue and Cosmopolitan.

Celebrity fans like Tyra Banks, Mariah Carey and Christina Aguilera have fuelled the brand's cult status, as has Sanrio's clever policy of never making too many of any one product. This means every Hello Kitty item is a limited edition, a collectible, which makes the brand one of the most eagerly sought after on internet auction sites like eBay.

Sanrio is also extremely cautious about brand extensions, wary not to flood the market with inappropriately positioned Hello Kitty products. Matching the brand's image to the right product, at the right time, has always been a key to Sanrio's success. Another important factor in the 'purity' of the Hello Kitty image is that it is just that – an image. She's not a character that has sprung from a cartoon, movie or book with a fully developed story. She exists only as an icon, and is all the more powerful, and timeless, as a result.

sanrio.com

Home House

A modern club which combines luxurious surroundings with excellent food and a casual, relaxed atmosphere

Home House is one of London's most exciting new clubs, fast gaining a reputation for being amongst the best in London. If you want to be in with the in-crowd, this is the place to go.

Opened in 1999, Home House is located in one of London's most famous town houses, an eighteenth century 'palazzo' designed by the legendary Scottish architect, Robert Adam. After lying derelict for ten years, the house was skilfully restored to its former neo-classical Georgian splendour, and now features some of the most impressive interiors to be found anywhere in the UK.

This latest incarnation, which has rapidly established itself as one of the world's leading private members' clubs, returns the house to its original purpose. It was designed by Adam as a 'party house' for the Countess of Home – a fabulously rich socialite who died in 1784. The historic house has also been occupied by the Earl of Grey (of tea fame) and the infamous spy, Anthony Blunt, in its time.

Home House represents a welcome breath of fresh air amongst London's private members' clubs, which are often stuffy, snobbish, charmless, overcrowded and hidebound by convention. Its modern services, exceptional restaurant, eighteen sumptuously appointed bedrooms, Turkish bath, health spa and eighteenth century garden are all designed to indulge Home House's eclectic mix of members.

The formula has worked, as Home House has become one of the chicest clubs in town, attracting style leaders such as Madonna, Cher, Mick Jagger, Vivienne Westwood, Lord Linley and Patrick Cox. It is now one of the most fashionable and opulent addresses in London – the place to meet, throw a glitzy party, schmooze business contacts or just be seen.

Its managing director, former Savoy Director Brian Clivaz, has succeeded in his aim of turning Home House into a modern form of a Parisian salon – a centre of fun and gossip for the fabulously glamorous and successful.

The real achievement of Home House – and the reason, perhaps, that the waiting list is over 1400 – is that it combines glamorous surroundings with an unpretentious, relaxed atmosphere. The experienced Clivaz has paid great attention to detail – such as excellent service – which creates an ideal environment in which Home House's members thrive.

The eclectic nature of the membership of Home House is reflected in the eccentric crocodile caricature that features in the club's logo, as well as in other communications, in decadent silver foiling. He stands tall and wears a crown, fashioned like that of the Countess of Home and rests an arm on a walking cane.

Home House is also in the enviable position of not needing to advertise – its reputation precedes it. Word of mouth amongst London's movers and shakers is enough to continually feed the waiting list.

homehouse.co.uk

HOPE & GLORY

Est. 1989

Traditional refinement, embracing
a classic feel with influences
from English heritage and style

Knitwear is not normally associated with coolness, either literally or metaphorically. But Hope & Glory made its name producing knits with an edge, more akin to the Avengers than Noel Edmonds. Since its humble beginnings in 1989, Hope & Glory has successfully managed to translate its hip post-Mod aesthetic into every area of men's fashion, including an expanding line of accessories. Over the past twelve years, the brand has grown organically and now has stores in Covent Garden, Nottingham and the Bluewater shopping centre. The brand also remains a favourite with men's magazines like FHM and GQ and has been described as the best kept menswear secret in England. In 2001 it was voted the fifth most trend-setting brand in the UK by Menswear magazine.

Hope & Glory was founded by Marc Schneiderman and Jo Hopcraft, who spotted a gap in the market for designer knitwear at affordable prices. Initially they ran the operation from their front room, and have continued to build the brand only as finances permit. Schneiderman and Hopcraft never wanted to be an overnight success, but instead have gradually built up the brand as and when it felt right.

This blend of limited distribution and carefully crafted designs gave Hope & Glory the image of a cult brand, which it still maintains today without fully tipping over into the mainstream. The company understands the dangers of over-distribution, carefully balancing its own-label stores with a small selection of well chosen

HOPE & GLORY

Est. 1989

retailers. Public relations and in-store marketing, rather than mainstream advertising, are used to communicate with the public in order to bolster the perception of affordable elitism.

But the real key to Hope & Glory's success lies in the clothes themselves, which are different and directional, while remaining highly wearable. Specialist fabrics, quirky details and reinterpretations of classic styles all quietly say 'fashion' without screaming 'victim'. Using retro inspired reference points the collections have a definite identity with a strong and individual signature.

Recently Hope & Glory has begun launching separately branded lines to reflect its different product areas – for example, the classically inspired Heritage label sits alongside Archive (jersey and fine gauge knitwear), Coton de Nimes (denim products) and Sports Apparel. The popularity of the label's formal shirts and semi tailored jacketing in 2001 also inspired the launch of the City range – a new outlet in the City of London will open in late 2002. Hope & Glory will offer more in the way of accessories in future collections – due to the success of previous items like the Venus holdall and Jupiter rucksack which garnered enthusiastic reviews.

Despite its softly-softly approach to expansion, it was hardly likely that Hope & Glory would remain a British secret forever, and the brand is now moving into the international marketplace. The brand recently made its debut in Italy, and is initially seeking a presence in only 30 outlets.

hopeandglory.co.uk

Jean Paul GAULTIER

Jean Paul Gaultier was born in 1952 in the Arceuil suburb of Paris. An only child, he was doted on by his mother and, perhaps more importantly, by his grandmother – a bohemian figure who ran a beauty parlour from her home, and whose love of music and movies was to have a significant influence on his work. Gaultier presented his first collection in 1976 and began to amaze the fashion world with his daring, cheeky and extravagant designs. By 1984, Gaultier shows were getting rave reviews and he was sporting a dyed blond crop, a striped sailor's sweater and Doc Marten's boots. Jean Paul Gaultier – the brand – was born.

Mixing the sexes, ideas and cultures, borrowing, changing and recycling without ever losing sight of a certain 'Haute Couture' idea of fashion: that is the style, the charm and the elegance of Jean Paul Gaultier fashion which is mirrored by Parfums Jean Paul Gaultier.

Gaultier launched his first fragrance, "Classique", in 1993 – literally getting under the skin of thousands of women. He wanted people to be able to wear his creations even closer to their skin so fragrance was a perfect avenue, as this is the first layer of 'clothing' that is put on. Inspiration for the fragrance came from the memories of his heroine – his grandmother. His recollections were of a delightful paradise where the scent of face powder mingled with that of the Folies Bergères.

The outer packaging of "Classique" is yet another provocative and contrasting gesture: a tin can. Shining in chrome splendour, it protects the woman inside. Within lies the now famous bust-bottle shaped like a woman's torso encased in an ultra feminine pink corset. This bottle has become an objet d'art, a sculpture in its own right.

In 1996, Gaultier created "Le Male", a fragrance combining sensitivity with solidity, classic lavender with the atmosphere of the barber's shops of yesterday. The can took on a gleaming 'gunmetal' colour and the blue male torso bottle sported the famous stripes of Jean Paul's sailor's top: modern man, a 21st century globetrotter, a gentleman explorer.

The latest fragrance is Fragile. It celebrates Gaultier's entry into the selective world of Haute Couture. Fragile represents a word to describe modern day woman – ambivalent and complex, unique and precious, but most importantly feminine and proud to show it. To envelop and protect the fragility of the bottle, Gaultier chose thick cardboard packaging, tied with strapping and bearing a seal. Fragile is stamped all over the box – as if it is transporting precious, delicate objects. In contrast, the interior is lined with gold leaf – a classic Gaultier touch.

Jean Paul
GAULTIER
"LE MALE"

The inspiration for the bottle again came from a childhood memory of fascinating snow domes. The bottle is shaped in this way, with its snowflakes replaced by gold glitter. A woman in a long black dress with matching three quarter length gloves stands in the centre and is showered in glitter as the bottle is shaken.

Gaultier's advertising is characteristically dramatic, with executions that leap off the page or screen. Campaigns have featured the photography of David La Chapelle and ultra-hip Jean-Baptiste Mondino, whose love of the sensual and glamorous mirrors Gaultier's own. Gaultier also utilises media relations to the full, and his sharp wit, unmistakable look and increasingly outrageous imagination have earned him acres of media coverage.

With a combination of Hollywood glamour and French romanticism, with a bit of cross-dressing thrown in for good measure, Gaultier has truly earned his reputation of being the original enfant terrible.

jeanpaulgaultier.com

JohnRocha

Beauty, sensuality and a blend of tradition and modernity are all John Rocha hallmarks but above all, the key to his work is simplicity

John Rocha has close and consistent associations with the image, atmosphere and textures of Ireland – so it is surprising to find that his background is exotic and resolutely non-Irish. Rocha was born in Hong Kong, his mother is from mainland China and his father is Portuguese. His first move was to London, in the 1970s, but he was inspired to visit Ireland while using Irish linen in his graduate collection. He has never looked back, and in the 1980s he moved to Dublin, where he has lived for 21 years with Odette, his wife and business associate.

Rocha's distinctive style reflects his surroundings as well as elements of Irish traditions. For example, his Spring/Summer 2001 collection was described as 'reflecting his love of the natural beauty of Donegal'. The following summer's clothes were said to be 'a modern take on traditional handcrafted garments'. Rocha finds that another bonus of living in Ireland is the sense of freedom it brings. The ability to take a step back and draw on a multitude of influences has shaped Rocha's distinctive identity.

Hand-painted textiles, knitwear, vintage linen, antique lace, rope, leather and silk – Rocha delights in taking raw, natural materials and traditional techniques, and bending them to his will. And while there is nothing stuffy or conventional in his approach – he is not above putting a digital print on a skirt, or slashing a chiffon sleeve – he ensures that his clothes are always eminently wearable.

Rocha was named British Designer of the Year in 1994. Since then has consolidated his position as a respected craftsman who combines the ethereal with the resolutely commercial, in contract to rebellious outsiders like Alexander McQueen, or the playful satirist like Jean-Paul Gaultier.

In 1997 Rocha began designing for Waterford Crystal – not only one of Ireland's best-known brands but one of the top five crystal brands in the world. The success of the range encouraged him to branch out into other media, and he scored another major hit when Dublin's Morrison Hotel, with an interior designed by Rocha, opened in 1999. In the same year Rocha designed the uniforms worn by all 5,000 Virgin Atlantic Airways ground and air staff.

The following winter, the Rocha name appeared in the even more unlikely surroundings of the Debenhams department store, where he launched five collections embracing clothing, accessories and housewares. This brought

the Rocha name to a much wider proportion of the population than his previous projects, and was featured in TV and print ads for Debenhams. This was a new level of exposure for the brand which, until this point, relied solely on PR within the fashion press, with the exception of a single ad that appeared in Vogue at the specific request of Rocha.

Other design projects have followed: in 2000 he joined forces with the design group Space to work on his first residential project, which transformed an abandoned 1930s Liverpool postal depot into apartments and penthouses. In 2001 Rocha began work on the Beacon Court business and lifestyle centre in Dublin.

Rocha's determination to continue expanding his design portfolio was signalled in 2000 by the creation of his own company, Three Moon Design. Rocha continues to develop in new directions with a contemporary jewellery range being launched in 2002.

Rocha's transformation from fashion visionary to a member of the design establishment was confirmed in February 2002, when John Rocha was made a Commander of the British Empire (CBE) by Her Majesty the Queen.

KANGOL

Quirky urban chic with attitude

Think Kangol and immediately you think of the hippest hats around – Kangol wearers exude effortless cool.

The brand that is now recognised globally began life in 1938, when Russian Jacques Henryk Spreiregen began making and branding his own berets in the Lake District. The brand name Kangol was allegedly put together using the K from silK, Knitting or Knitted, the ANG from angora and the OL from wool.

The mid 1950s saw the introduction of what is now seen as the ultimate homeboy accessory, the 504 cap; and as Kangol began to grow it extended into women's designs. During the 1960s, the brand was embraced by movers and shakers including the Beatles, Mary Quant and Pierre Cardin.

The now familiar kangaroo icon wasn't introduced until 1983. The move was prompted by the surge of interest in Kangol hats in the US to the extent that imitators were entering the market. Many Americans had been going into shops asking for 'kangaroo' hats and caps. So instead of trying to re-educate the entire nation, the kangaroo was adopted clearly differentiating the Kangol brand as the headwear leader.

With a firm grip on the hats market, Kangol began developing in new directions during the 1990s, diversifying and growing the brand to include clothing, footwear, bags and eyewear.

It has maintained its status by a continued inspiration from constantly evolving British society – linking with music and street culture. Kangol's philosophy is to celebrate the diversity of the modern nation and its people. By having an understanding of the many different strands of Britishness, the brand has an advantage when competing with the rest of the world.

Kangol has deliberately avoided heavy reliance on traditional advertising. On the rare occasions it has advertised, exposure is limited to a select group of style magazines. Instead it prefers to create awareness through association, using PR and activities that allow it to communicate in a subtle way that the target audience appreciates. The likes of its music and photographic campaign with Dazed and Confused does just that. Kangol has also introduced a fresh new website so it can get closer to its wearers and issues relevant to them.

Celebrity endorsements have long been central to this strategy. LL Cool J sported a Kangol Bermuda Casual on his debut album, Radio, spawning a hip new audience and anchoring Kangol at the core of a movement as the hip-hop phenomenon grew. Samuel L Jackson wore a variety of 504 caps throughout the whole of Quentin Tarantino's Jackie Brown.

Inspired by the colours of the Union Jack (but jumbled up a bit, like Kangol Britain), the entire Kangol brand is now broken down into three sections – White, Red and Blue. Blue includes Kangol's heritage collection, featuring re-invented classics from the Kangol archives. Red signifies youthful, colourful experimentation – Red wearers spend life on the edge, are thrill-seekers and solo action junkies.

White is the directional expression of Kangol. Keeping an eye on the fast-moving world of fashion, these designs are created in collaboration with Britain's brightest design talent on a seasonal basis. Kangol pioneered this project in 2000 with Katharine Hamnett. Since then, Bella Freud, YMC, 6876, Antoni + Alison, and Heather Allan have all made their individual interpretations of Kangol's signature pieces.

The continued success of the Kangol approach is confirmed by ongoing approval from the fashion elite – not least by celebrity wearers both in the UK and stateside with the likes of Jude Law, De La Soul, Outkast, Guy Ritchie, Macy Gray and Limp Bizkit to name but a few.

kangol.com

Lambretta

Lambrete, Milan 1947. This was the setting for the launch of Ferdinando Innocenti's 123cc engine scooter. The Lambretta, named after the town of its conception, was an instant hit with the Italians. So much so that Ferdinando soon began exporting the scooter across the world. In 1951 the first Lambretta hit British shores and by 1959 the brand was outstripping sales of Vespas – scooters that were already established in the UK. With ideal timing the 1960s arrived and with them came British mod culture. A need for rebellion took hold of the country's youth. Mods and Rockers went to war, fuelled by their opposing taste in music, clothing and lifestyles. And how better for Mods to chase Rockers than on their Lambrettas. Despite its Italian origins, the Lambretta brand had by now adopted a very English personality: the Union Jack and the scooters went hand in hand.

The Lambretta scooter is now no longer in production, but the Lambretta brand and its values live on. Still embedded at the heart of youth culture, Lambretta clothing has become one of the most sought after fashion labels in the UK and abroad. Lambretta launched as a clothing label in 1997 and is now renowned for its retro inspired collections.

Lambretta's flagship store opened on Carnaby Street in 1997; it then expanded with the opening of a further store in the Victoria Quarter, Leeds, which was followed by a third in Covent Garden, London, which opened in February 2002.

The atmospherics of the stores provide a stylish, airy and contemporary showcase for the Lambretta collections and are painted in the signature Lambretta 'Mint' green. The Covent Garden store also features fixtures in a Gun Metal finish, with frosted glass shelving. All the stores contain a unique custom-made Union Jack sofa and a scooter, but unique to the Covent Garden store is the fact that the scooter is changed every three months for a different model.

Originally launched as a menswear label, Lambretta introduced a women's range in 1999 which has also proved to be a success. Lambretta has recently followed this with a range of men's suiting, which includes a collection of shirts and ties.

Lambretta's patriotic World Cup Collection, which hit the stores in April 2002, consisted of track tops, pique shirts, football as target logo t-shirts, coat of arms t-shirts and sweatshirts. To tie in with this, Lambretta's promotional activity for 2002 is based around football. Advertisements,

which were shot on the pitch at Millwall football club, are running in FHM collections, Loaded Fashion, Maxim Fashion, i-D, The Face, Sleazenation and Four Four Two magazines. In addition, pitchside boards are being used at televised premiership matches, FA Cup matches and Worthington Cup matches. Lambretta also supplied all the clothing for the video of the World Cup single 'Standing Tall' by 'Bubble & Deano' of Big Brother fame. The brand also sponsors up and coming bands.

To both reinforce its youthful credentials and get noticed, Lambretta also provides clothing for staff at selected bars and clubs throughout the UK.

lambrettaclothing.co.uk

ⓂANUMISSION

Manumission is about freeing people from the slavery of their everyday lives and taking them into a world of pure pleasure. In fact, the name itself is derived from the Latin meaning 'freedom from slavery'. Manumission has done this and revolutionised the party scene in the process. Rather than focusing simply on music, its inspiration is drawn from further afield and elements of cabaret, theatre and the arts are incorporated in the sixteen events that are held in Ibiza each summer.

Manumission was created by brothers Andy and Mike McKay in Manchester in 1994 with the vision of being a straight and gay friendly night that they would have liked to go to themselves but couldn't find in the club scene at that time. Violence then began to flare in the Manchester club scene, so when the brothers went on holiday to Ibiza, they were struck by how the paradise island reflected Manumissions mind set of freedom and expression. They then decided to take Manumission to this island of extremes.

Producing flyers and posters that simply said 'Manumission is coming', the opening night brought many more people than could fit into the venue and by the time the fifth party was held, 6,000 people were turning up – a far cry from the brothers nights at the 400-capacity club in Manchester. Manumission's reputation continued to grow not only through that season, but when it returned the following year. Its success subsequently led to the superclubs, such as Ministry of Sound, opening in Ibiza.

Manumission rewrote the rule book by introducing door fees of £30. Previously admission to clubs had been free with club owners making money through the sale of drinks. Rivals thought a fee would drive customers away but the income meant that the McKays could transform the level of entertainment on offer.

A full theatrical management team was employed and a cast of up to 200 people now performs at each event. In the early days live sex shows were introduced at the club, gaining worldwide notoriety. But when rivals began

> The biggest party in the world with an exceptional and fantastical ambience

Photography by Victor Spinelli

to follow suit, Manumission moved on. It is constantly evolving and no two summers are ever the same. Past years themes have included Manumission the Movie, The Good Ship Manumission, Manumission the World Series and in 2002, Manumission Ibithan Myths. The sets are designed by Mark Fisher, who has produced shows for many of the world's leading bands, such as U2.

Unlike other clubs, Manumission fiercely protects its brand. Three years ago, it took the decision to stop promoting superstar DJs, recognising that at rival clubs the DJs were becoming more famous than the clubs that created them. It's a move that has paid off. Manumission's customers are more interested in the party atmosphere than who is on the decks.

Manumission doesn't advertise in the press because they believe that the best form of advertising is word of mouth. Instead the parties are promoted using street processions, beach parades and guerrilla

marketing techniques. The money saved on campaigns is ploughed back into making the events even more spectacular.

Manumission, which is still a small family-owned business run by Andy, Mike and their partners Dawn Hindle and Claire Davies has resisted the temptation to tour or return to the UK. It limits the number of parties it holds and spends all year preparing for them. While other club brands have expanded into other areas such as records and festivals, Manumission focuses on its core activity and continues to attract 8,000 hedonists a week. The Manumission team does however run bar m – the most successful pre club bar in Ibiza.

Such is its success that, according to the Guinness Book of Records, Manumission is now the biggest party in the world.

manumission.com

Mercedes-Benz

A fusion of glamour and luxury plus the highest standards of safety, quality and innovation

The Mercedes-Benz brand conjures up images of motoring luxury, quality and performance. Indeed, the brand has been responsible for producing some of the world's most stylish performance cars.

The common values of all Mercedes-Benz cars are superb design and engineering, together with a sense of heritage. The name Emil Jellinek probably won't ring any bells but his ten year old daughter Mercedes will. In 1898 Karl Benz designed a new car for Jellinek to compete in the 'Nice Race' that year and on Jellinek's request, it was named after his daughter, Mercedes.

The famous Mercedes-Benz star logo came about after Karl Benz sent his wife a postcard with a star marking out the house where he was living in Deutz, Germany. "One day this star will shine down on my work", he wrote.

In 1909 a trademark was taken out on the star, the three points of which have come to symbolize the threefold nature of motor transport – by land, sea and air. They have also come to represent what the brand stands for: service and safety and all over the world, a pioneering spirit and tradition.

Racing has always been in the brand's blood and indeed was responsible for the formation of Mercedes-Benz in the first place. Back in 1924, after winning 269 races between them, Daimler and Benz, up to that point competing companies, opted to cooperate and merged their operations into the present day Mercedes-Benz.

Innovation and dramatic styling is also part of the company's tradition. 1952 saw the introduction of the futuristic, gull-wing doored 300 SL; a dream car from the moment it made its first appearance. With a top speed of over 150 mph, it was the first of the famous SL-Class models. On the race track, the car was a huge success, leading to the creation of the 190SL,

Consider your prayers answered

Mercedes-Benz

a 'popular' and more affordable version. The pedigree line has continued to this day with the current generation of SL roadsters that epitomise head-turning elegance as much as sportiness on the road. The line continues with the SLK-Class, unveiled as a 'concept car' at the 1994 Turin Motor Show to a rapturous welcome. A new SL-Class was launched in April 2002 in the UK and the SLR will be launched in 2003.

The other facets of the Mercedes-Benz personality – safety and technical innovation – are hugely important to the brand. Mercedes was the first in the world to fit a four-valve diesel engine in a car to offer enhanced performance, smoothness and extreme longevity. In addition, as early as 1961, the company started to fit anchorage points for seat belts as standard. Mercedes also pioneered ABS braking, the airbag, pre-tensioning devices and the passenger safety cell.

The innovative Mercedes-Benz A-Class heralded a new generation of relatively small vehicles which boast the abilities of larger ones in finding space for people and luggage, but in a pleasingly compact frame. The A-Class has also attracted a younger group of people to the Mercedes-Benz brand, with more relaxed lifestyle values than the traditional Mercedes-Benz owner. The stylish 'Oh Lord, won't you buy me a Mercedes-Benz' TV and print campaign helped to introduce a new generation of people to the brand, as well as reflecting its aspirational qualities. In addition, Mercedes continues to sponsor carefully selected events which reflect the brand's values.

Mercedes-Benz occupies a position at the pinnacle of the motor industry and the brand still represents 'dream car' status amongst a new generation of drivers.

Cutting-edge streetwear for men and women

Moist was founded in 1993 by Jeremy Foster and David Kellard in a mad moment when they were offered space in an empty shop. The duo recognised the importance and strength of the youth market and decided to stock the small outlet with t-shirts, hooded sweatshirts and music products such as tapes and record bags for dance music enthusiasts and early urban surfers.

The pair's choice of a slightly risky name for the fledgling brand reflected its cheeky youthful nature – definitely not the kind of branded shopping bag your mother would want to be seen carrying.

As support for Moist grew, so did its product range, maintaining its individuality by stocking little-known, cutting edge, urban streetwear brands such as Hooch, Bench, Two Legs, Go Vicinity, Addict, Komodo, Pash, Map, Kronk, DNA, Blunt and Traffic. Now Moist has grown into a successful chain of six shops, all located

in the south of England. Moist has received many accolades, for example, the Brighton store was given the award for 'Best Clothes Shop In Brighton 2001' by Impact Magazine and Juice FM.

The majority of Moist's customers are between 15-23 years old. However, Moist also appeals to older fashion-conscious adults – the original Moist customers who have moved on in many ways but still shop at Moist.

It is very important to Moist that each store retains its own culture and personality. To achieve this, the manager of each shop has a certain level of autonomy that allows them to recruit their own staff and manage their own working environment. In addition, the music played in the shops is chosen by the staff, there is no rigid corporate structure, no closed office doors, and no uniforms or specific shop fittings.

The fluid nature of the brand is enhanced by the encouragement given to each shop to evolve at its own pace, remaining unique and independent and reflecting the environment around it.

The shops also maintain their freshness by constantly updating stock so that customers will always find something new and different when they visit.

Moist is different from other clothing chains as it buys stock and sells it within the same season, always on the look out for the next shift in style.

A benefit of having a small chain is that each shop can be given ample attention and the staff are treated as individuals. From the very beginning, honest and friendly relationships with suppliers have been encouraged and bills have been paid on time without fail – something of a rarity in the business. This has ensured a good reputation in the trade, encouraging suppliers to approach Moist first with new products. Particular attention has been given to suppliers who have a good ethical policy on garment production.

The brand is only promoted in student magazines and at underground events or sponsored club nights to keep it out of the mainstream and reflect its underground, independent characteristics.

MUSIC TELEVISION®

From the moment The Buggles' 'Video Killed the Radio Star' launched MTV, music's coolest television channel, a hip musical revolution was born. That moment was August 1st 1981. Just six months later, the channel had over two million US subscribers – attracted not only by the music but also by the strikingly glossy and trendy presenters. During the 1980s and early 1990s, the first MTV Video Music Awards were aired, Michael Jackson's 'Thriller' video was premiered, Live Aid was broadcast to the US public and some incredible prizes, including a tropical island, Madonna's gold conical Jean Paul Gaultier bra and Billy Idol's Harley Davidson, were won by viewers. By 1991, the channel was available in 27 countries.

A lifeline to popular culture worldwide

Following the success of MTV in the US, MTV Europe launched on August 1st 1987 in Amsterdam; the first video shown was 'Money for Nothing' by Dire Straits, which included the infamous line, 'I want my MTV'. The channel's first birthday was celebrated with 3.5 million subscribers and spread to Germany, Belgium, Switzerland, Greece and Norway. By the end of the year, it was available in 6.7 million homes. In 1994 the MTV Europe Music Awards were born and broadcast live from Berlin. These awards have now become the most watched music awards ceremony in the world with an audience of over one billion. The Europe Music Awards delivered MTV's highest ever rating in the UK in 2001, and had more than two million people voting on the website and via the MTV Interactive service.

The need for localised territory feeds saw the launch of MTV UK & Ireland in 1997. mtv.co.uk launched and is now the biggest music website in the UK. Working at the cutting edge of technology to deliver music more innovatively, MTV UK has maintained its pole position through pioneering programmes such as Videoclash, an interactive show that combines live TV with mobile phone texting. Its interactive marketing campaign was a finalist for Media Week's Best Interactive Campaign Award in 2001 and in the Campaign Media Awards for Best Use of New Media for Consumers. MTV's events also reflect its passion for pop as well as other music styles. Its Five Night Stand, which took place early in 2002, gave viewers the chance to see bands

Warning: THE OSBOURNES CAN BE HIGHLY ADDICTIVE

Sundays at 10pm

MTV is available on Sky (440), ntl:home, Telewest Broadband, ITV Digital or your local cable operator
mtv.co.uk/theosbournes

as diverse as Blue and Super Furry Animals in intimate venues over five nights.

MTV Networks UK now has seven channels covering a huge spectrum of music genres: MTV, MTV Hits, MTV Dance, MTV Base, MTV2, VH1 and VH1 Classic.

MTV is supported by many major recording artists, who use it as a means of communication. Michael Jackson chose MTV to make his comeback at the Video Music Awards 2001, Eminem's first interview in the UK was on MTV, and Madonna announced her first European tour in eight years on the channel.

Offering its audience programmes that embrace popular culture, MTV is currently available in 92 million homes across Europe and a massive 340 million worldwide (spanning 140 countries). There's not a shred of doubt: MTV brings music to the masses.

mtv.co.uk

It is hard to believe that a brand as radically cool – and internationally successful – as Oakley grew out of something as simple as a handlebar grip. But that is how the company's tough CEO Jim Jannard started out at the age of just 25, designing a new grip because he felt those he was selling as a motorcycle accessories sales rep just weren't good enough. He started his company with an initial investment of $300 and named it after his dog. Today he is a billionaire.

Jannard's first 'eureka' moment happened when he invented Unobtanium, a synthetic material that actually provides a better grip when wet. He designed his grips

An original, unexpected and innovative world brand

to ergonomically fit the human hand, and finished them off with an 'octopus' tread pattern that made them even less likely to slip through sweat-damp palms. He toted them around the motocross circuit, where they quickly developed a devoted following. Jannard then – in the first display of a career-long talent for spotting the right niche – turned his attention to the BMX market, where his grips were even more successful and became cult favourites with riders. However, Oakley remained virtually unknown to outsiders, as exposure beyond those circles was very limited.

The Oakley boss then worked out how to get more exposure for his brand. He designed a pair of goggles, the Oakley O Frame, employing cutting edge technology that virtually guaranteed they would be used by the stars of the Motocross and BMX industry, so he had the Oakley brand printed clearly on the strap for maximum media exposure.

During the 1980s, Oakley evolved from a provider of cutting edge sport-specific goggles and sunglasses, designed with athletes in mind, into an eyewear brand with great crossover potential. Inevitably the worlds of BMX and snowboarding bled into the street fashion market. Jannard simply stuck to his own maxim: find an opportunity, solve it with technology, and wrap it in art.

Another turning point in the brand's history came in 1995, when Jannard took the company public. The blend of advanced technology, athlete support and cutting edge designs proved successful and drove the brand forward.

Oakley is now a global lifestyle brand, selling sunglasses, clothing, watches and footwear to 18-34 year olds in 70 countries.

Oakley has continuously focused on supporting athletes that reflect the brand's youthful, cutting edge style. By establishing strong athlete relationships these core ambassadors of sport have endorsed and legitimised the Oakley brand.

Oakley is a favourite amongst a wide array of athletes, from cyclist Lance Armstrong to snowboarder Terje Haakonsen, but has also found a following amongst film stars. For example, Tom Cruise wore Oakley shades in Mission Impossible II and Wesley Snipes also wore them in Blade II. Oakley continues to drive the brand forward through advertising within leading sport and style publications, with focused, relevant and visually powerful advertising aimed at cutting edge sports enthusiasts.

Innovation and technology have remained at the heart of the brand. Oakley has invented and patented materials to surpass many industry

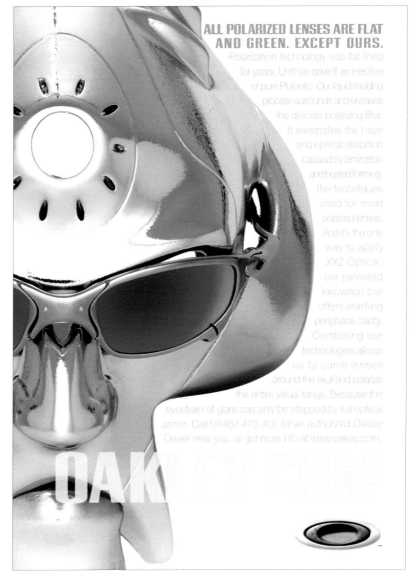

standards in all of its product areas. In eyewear, innovations include Plutonite, from which Oakley lenses are made – an optically pure polycarbonate that provides 100% protection against UVA, UVB, UVC and harmful blue light. In footwear, from the early Carbon Fibre and Kevlar enhanced breakaway styles, Oakley has introduced new revolutionary processes such as Netshape Technology, which has allowed the use of CAD/CAM engineering to make every component fit exactly.

oakley.com

OLYMPUS

The British NickDanziger

OLYMPUS CAMERAS

The British, a collection of photographs by Nick Danziger,
taken from his book of the same title, will be on view at the
following Fullers pubs for 3 weeks from October 12th:

The Old Bank of England, Fleet Street

Barrow Boy & Banker, London Bridge

The Counting House, Cornhill

Butchers Hook & Cleaver, West Smithfield

Melton Mowbray, Holborn

Shooting Star, Bishopsgate

FULLERS

People have always felt the desire to capture images of events
or moments that might otherwise be forgotten. There are
many brands of camera to satisfy this urge, but it takes
something special to encapsulate the style and glamour
of photography. Thanks to a rich heritage of innovative,
consistently focused marketing, Olympus has achieved a
chicness to which few other technology brands can aspire.
In a crowded and homogenous market, Olympus has, for
over 80 years, successfully carved a distinctive and clearly
differentiated brand position.

Olympus has generated years of groundbreaking
creative work and professional endorsements. The memorable
1970s TV commercials starring the legendary photographer
David Bailey made a huge impact. The fact that the name
of the brand promoted in those ads – the Olympus Trip
– is still top of mind sixteen years after the adverts were
on TV is a testament to the campaign's impact on popular
culture. The easy-to-use Trip makes quality photography
accessible to the masses – a contribution which should
not be undervalued.

Ads that themselves have generated a cult following have
always helped build the iconic status of the Olympus brand.
The famous David Bailey commercials were followed by
other campaigns, using carefully chosen figureheads who,
like Olympus, are style leaders. Sandra Bernhard, Joan Collins
and Naomi Campbell are just three examples.

Olympus has also made intelligent use of sponsorship and
PR to nurture its reputation for creativity and style. Its long-

running support of the Fashion Acts exhibition, in which celebrities use Olympus cameras to create images which are then auctioned for charity, has become an established feature of the London art and fashion scene. Another initiative underlining Olympus's special brand of cool is its sponsorship of 'The British' – a collection of images by photographer Nick Danziger. These pictures were exhibited in some of Britain's most popular locations, reaching a broad section of the public, namely in selected Fullers pubs throughout London.

In addition, continuing its long-standing relationship with David Bailey, Olympus recently sponsored 'Insiders' for the Big Issue – a study by the legendary photographer of prison inmates.

Of course, Olympus is not only a brand that leads the way in terms of style and glamour. Most important is that it also has a peerless reputation for technological innovation; constantly creating products which change the way we record and live our lives. The impact of Olympus is all around us – for example, it invented Taos, the laser optical pickup found in every CD player. Now it is leading the field in digital photography, designing cameras that, like the Trip, make the latest technology truly easy to use and accessible.

Olympus has been developing key messages and activities to demonstrate the new digital technology to a new market. By showing products and enabling hands on experience at youth orientated events Olympus is ensuring a brand experience at all levels. The diverse range of activities including presence at Urban Games, B Boy breakdancing championships and at the Clothes Show Live.

Like many of Olympus's activities, its about building for the future, an example of how the brand remains ahead of the competition.

OLYMPUS
DIGITAL CAMERAS

olympus.co.uk

Opium

From the moment you enter the gold tunnel entrance leading to the dimly-lit confines of Opium's principal room, your senses are indulged in a feast of exotic splendour.

Opium was created and conceptualised by entrepreneur Eric Yu – who was voted Most Influential Individual 2001 by industry bible Theme magazine. He is the chairman of the Breakfast Group, which also includes star venues Jerusalem, Pop, The Social and Grand Central in its portfolio.

Thanks to the vision of Miguel Cancio Martins, the Paris-based designer behind cool Parisian hotspots Buddha Bar, Bar Fly and Man Ray,

Opium is a fashionable Vietnamese bar and restaurant in London's Soho. It has a truly opulent interior that has already earned it the award of Best New Venue at the Bacardi London Club and Bar Awards 2001.

Opium has been designed with attention to detail being paramount. Ornate wooden screens, bespoke French furniture, relaxing sofas, sultry lighting and a winter garden all help to create the underground, 'opium den' vibe the clientele have been addicted to since Opium opened in November 2000. The design detail on menus, matchboxes, cloakroom tokens and specially commissioned fans have been created to blend with their surroundings and feel like part of the interior whilst adding to the total Opium experience. The cocktail menus are designed like a swatch book with staggered pages that open upwards rather than outwards. The cloakroom tokens are in fact ornate beaded bands, which are such beautiful objects in themselves they often get stolen. Opium fans, another individual touch, are given out to female visitors. In addition, the Opium logo was specifically hand drawn to reflect and tie in with the individuality of the hand made furnishings which are apparent throughout the interior.

As Vietnam was a French colony for many years, the food at Opium has embraced rather than shunned French culinary influences, lending a distinctly 'Indochine' fusion feel to the cuisine. Unlike many other Oriental eateries, the food is served European-style as single dishes, as opposed to being shared in the middle of the table, and an added bonus is that the menu is extremely health-conscious – the chefs use less oil than many other Asian menus.

With exotic juices and herbs being the preferred ingredients, the bar's cocktails have gained a reputation for their cutting-edge originality. Divided into four groups – Frosts, Frappes, Longs and Martinis – star creations include white chocolate martinis and Cua Lo Frost: raspberry rice wine, creme de Framboise and fresh raspberry topped with Rose champagne.

The perfect soundtrack is essential to complement the laid-back, loungey atmosphere, and the venue's choice of sophisticated world music rarely disappoint. Live performances from various 'Chanteuses' performing a repertoire of French torch songs plus exclusive sets from Paris-based DJ's Claude Challe and DJ Albert, who fly in on Saturdays to play, take the mood from chilled to more upbeat as the evening progresses.

Opium has rapidly been recognised as a 'must visit' pitstop on the world circuit and continues to grow in popularity through word of mouth. It has also become a popular celebrity hang out, with a guest list including the likes of George Clooney, Lisa Snowdon, Kate Moss, Jay Kay, Patsy Kensit, Yasmin & Simon Le Bon, Jade Jagger, Liv Tyler, Mick Jagger, Stella McCartney, Liza Minnelli, David Ginola, Eric Cantona and Miuccia Prada.

opium-bar-restaurant.com

In 1992 two entrepreneurs, Christian Arden and
Rob Sawyer, set up a Moroccan-themed bar
called Po Na Na on London's fashionable King's
Road. It was based on a bar that Sawyer had
once visited in LA and never forgotten. Run
by two French Algerians and filled with North
African artefacts, it had conjured up the spirit
of the souk.

Arden and Sawyer set about recreating that
atmosphere and Po Na Na Souk Bar, meaning
'magical market bar' in Arabic, was launched as
a chilled out alternative to the vast superclubs
and bland chain-pubs on offer.

Whilst not
pretending to emulate
an authentic north
African restaurant, the
sites evoke images of
exotic medinas and
heady nights. Clever
use of space defines
the bars, open areas
are enclosed into
intimate alcoves,
with textiles, Moorish
furniture, ironwork
and artefacts used
to stunning effect.
Lanterns diffuse light
onto ceilings and floors,
whilst the many levels
for seating and lounging
ensure a relaxing environment throughout the
night but keep distinct music/dance areas for
those that wish to party.

The brand itself has a slightly mischievous
air, embodied in Po Na Na's logo, a winking,
Fez-wearing man with a cheeky grin.

From the beginning, Po Na Na has attracted
a range of celebrities from Robbie Williams and
Kylie Minogue to Mick Jagger, and has pulled off

ponana.co.uk

that rare feat of being consistently popular without being over-hyped. It has now grown from a single venue to become the largest independent operator of late night bars in the UK. It attracts over 100,000 customers a week and has a turnover of £30 million a year. It has assiduously colonised university towns, and areas with a credible music oriented customer base. In harnessing the individual talents, local knowledge and musical diversity of its staff and managers Arden and Sawyer have managed to create a concept that is unique in every town and city.

A major part of the attraction of Po Na Na is its music policy, which spans a variety of genres from global dance to jazz, Latin to reggae as well as pop classics. It seeks out and hosts the latest in cutting edge music trends and this year launched the first Po Na Na branded CD. 'Door to the Souk' is an eclectic compilation capturing the exoticism of North Africa, Cuba and Brazil, inspired by the vibrancy and ambience of Po Na Na. In keeping with its credible music policy, Po Na Na launched a nationwide tour in 2002 called Hedflux, the essence of which took big named artists such as Mr Scruff, Cut la Roc, and Gilles Peterson to name a few and hosted them in its small intimate venues. The tour has been such a success that another is planned for later in 2002.

Most recently the company acquired the famous Hammersmith Palais, and renamed it Po Na Na Hammersmith. It hosts the phenomenally successful Schooldisco, which attracts 2,500 revellers a week dressed in Britney Spears style school uniform. The company has also made successful partnerships abroad – venues have already opened in Barbados, Cape Town and St. Anton and others are in the pipeline. Po Na Na's Moroccan Tent Company will launch shortly and take the brand into festivals and outdoor events as well as private hire.

The Po Na Na philosophy is not 'one style fits all' – each is created as an individual experience not a bar chain. Arden and Sawyer are fully aware of the value of Po Na Na as a youth brand and anticipate wider use of the brand across related markets in the years ahead.

Red Stripe, the laid-back cult lager

From Leeds to London, urban style-junkies, music moguls and party animals are turning to cult lagers such as Red Stripe to fuel their hectic leisure time. Nowadays as much as 30% of all consumer spend on alcohol in the UK is on beer.

Red Stripe was first brewed in Kingston, Jamaica back in the 1920s – its name is thought to have been inspired by the stripes on the trousers of Jamaica's policemen – and went into full production in 1934. Paul Geddes, the man behind the brand, developed the globally praised, distinctive combination of crisp drinkability and subtle strength by blending imported yeast and hops from Washington State's Yakima Valley in the US.

In 1976 Red Stripe was introduced into the UK and with it came its laid back Jamaican attitude and the first licence to brew Red Stripe anywhere other than Jamaica. Keeping a check on its authentic Jamaican roots, Red Stripe was soon introduced in draught form to the same specification, quality and strength as the bottle format, and is now one of Europe's fastest growing premium lager beers. Since then, Red Stripe has grown from a 7,000 barrel brand to producing over 120,000 a year.

Fast-forward to the new millennium and the rebirth of Red Stripe and its cool, cult status. Red Stripe was repackaged in 2001 with a redesigned can and a stubbie bottle, which replicates the one sold in Jamaica and replaced the original long neck bottle. Red Stripe's advertising was key to its reinvention, with quirky amusing ads establishing an equally challenging personality.

Red Stripe, like the people who drink it, also realised that lager and music go together very well. The brand established firm links with a wide variety of music styles and venues.

Old fashioned barber pole style light boxes sporting the Red Stripe logo can now be found at some of the best urban music venues across the country. These venues include the Brixton, Birmingham and Bristol Academies, Shoreditch Electricity Showrooms and The Yard in London and Prague V and Barça bar in Manchester. Red Stripe's commitment to live, digital and recorded music in the UK is continually reinforced by sponsorship campaigns, including previous associations with the Notting Hill Carnival and the Knowledge Drum & Bass Awards as well as constant and consistent immersion in all aspects of music, club and bar culture.

Red Stripe's website also plays an important part in communicating its links with the urban music scene with nationwide gig and club listings as well as offering a free download of ReBirth music creation software.

The success of Red Stripe is reflected by the fact that it is one of Europe's fastest growing premium beers. In tandem with this, Red Stripe's superior quality has been recognised through the five gold medals it has won in each of the five open lager competitions it has entered over an eighteen month period.

Nice 'im up *Red Stripe*

sleazenation

Rip Off *Red Stripe*

redstripe.net

Slot car racing with the best cars in motor sport

Is there any other slot racing brand apart from Scalextric? An enthusiast could probably tell you – but for the rest of us, the image of minutely detailed cars whizzing around a track as we jostle for elbow space with our dads is fused with this one name.

As well as continuing to capture the imaginations of pre-teens (and their parents), Scalextric has benefited from the rise in popularity of Formula One, a significant collectors' market, and the thirty something – largely male – passion for retro kitsch. Add to that the fact that video games have made leisure pursuits previously reserved for children perfectly acceptable to adults, and you have a strong marketing proposition.

Scalextric is owned by a brand more closely associated with model trains – Hornby, founded by Frank Hornby, who also invented Meccano. But the brand was originally developed by a company called Minimodels, which in 1952 began producing clockwork cars under the name Scalex. By the late 1950s this evolved into a track-based electric system and the brand became Scalextric. In the late 1960s the launch of a banked figure-of-eight circuit was a turning point for the brand, as it immediately proved popular. In addition, cars became even more detailed – up to the point of printing insignia directly onto the bodies, rather than using transfers.

Now Scalextric is the pre-eminent name in slot car racing, aided by its continuing focus on accuracy. Cars are often based on the original prototypes of the vehicles that inspired them, with Computer Aided Design replicating even the tiniest details. And the system continues to evolve. Scalextric recently introduced its Sport Advanced Track System, the first major change to the track in over 40 years. It is flatter, smoother, quicker to assemble and has a deeper slot – combating the familiar problem of cars sailing off the track. New cars made specifically for the system feature ground axles and brass bearings to create smoother running and an even better grip.

Scalextric can now be found as a pulse racing edition to parties and as after dinner entertainment. Eight lane tracks have been specially designed to allow drivers to play at the same time, with a computerised start and timing system keeping the races in order.

For promotional purposes, Scalextric depends a great deal on its website, which offers news from the full-scale motor racing world, as well as details of new products and the ability to order kit. Ingenious advances like the downloadable Scalextric Sport Race Management System recreate the atmosphere of a genuine motor racing championship, monitoring circuit times and fuel levels.

Scalextric are teaming up with Ford and the Focus On World Rally Roadshow to launch a competition to find a champion Scalextric Sport racer. The Scalextric Sport Challenge will take place at Ford Focus World Rally Roadshow venues across the UK from May to November 2002.

Scalextric has survived a lot of competition in its time – vying for attention over the years with new toys – but the thrill of having a racetrack in your bedroom still creates a buzz.

scalextric.com

SELFRIDGES&Cº

> The ultimate modern day emporium, offering a stylish mix of products ranging from furniture to fashion, beauty and food

Selfridges is a retail experience. Even before entering the store, the innovative window displays – designed by the in house marketing team who have previously worked in collaboration with Rankin, Ron Arad and Uli Weber – give you an idea of the cutting edge chic within. Vittorio Radice, Selfridges' 45 year old Milan-born Chief Executive, describes walking into the store as akin to going on holiday – you leave your troubles at the door and enter a fantasy world.

The store sells over one million products and is packed with designer brands. Everything Selfridges sells can be described simply as an impulse purchase. Radice has indeed said, "You won't find anything in the store you desperately need to survive: it's about extras to make your life better."

Selfridges is about life's intangibles too and, with its unerring ability to tap into the Zeitgeist, Selfridges launched a Health and Wellbeing department in 2001. This includes Farmacia Urban Healing, an integrated pharmacy and natural health clinic that offers conventional and complementary therapies and treatment, and the high-tech Ora Dental Suite where you can have your teeth whitened while watching the latest Hollywood video release.

Selfridges renaissance is not just about the things it sells. Contemporary art and architecture has given the store a facelift. Christian Liagre added a deeply glamorous sparkle to the huge cosmetics hall and Ron Arad created the Technology Hall – a futuristic, high-tech interactive showcase for a raft of state of the art consumer technology products.

Nowhere is Selfridges' intuitive and innovative approach to design more evident than in the store's major promotions, which are pure retail theatre and attract the attention of both customers and the media. The wide-ranging, month-long Tokyo Life promotion in May 2001 transformed the store

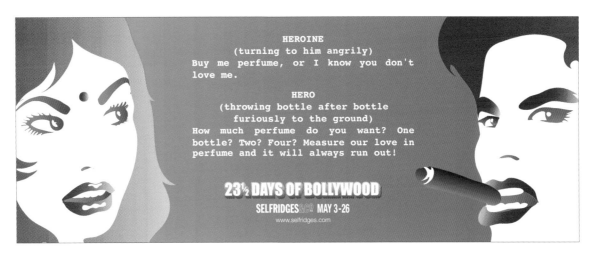

into a grand celebration of Japanese commerce and culture.

The store was taken over again in May 2002 with the largest promotion to date when Selfridges played host to '23 1/2 Days of Bollywood', the biggest celebration ever mounted of Bollywood's film culture with over 60 live events as well as appearances by Bollywood star names – Amitabh Bachchan, Dimple Kapadia, Madhuri Dixit and Hritik Roshan.

Radice, who doubled Habitat's turnover in three years before moving to Selfridges in 1996, believes that most people who go shopping are really just out for a walk and buy on impulse. He drew inspiration from Gordon Selfridge, the US entrepreneur who left his job in 1909 at the famous Chicago retailer Marshall Fields to launch his own business in England. Selfridge saw the department store as a vibrant centre at the heart of urban life – a kind of microcosm of a major city offering a myriad of experiences to a diversity of people.

In keeping with the founder's vision, Selfridges has plans to create an additional 100,000 square feet of retail space in Oxford Street as well as adding a contemporary hotel, restaurant and replacement car park. What's more, the brand is becoming more accessible to trend-hungry urbanites outside London: in 1998 Selfridges opened a second store in Manchester's Trafford Centre, a third store will open in Manchester's Exchange Square in September 2002, and a fourth, with a daring futuristic design by Future Systems, will open in Birmingham in 2003.

To set the seal on its success, Selfridges won the Time Out Retail Award in 2001 for The Best Department Store and in the same year, Management Today judged it to be one of Britain's ten most admired companies. In 2002, Selfridges also won the Glamour magazine award for The Most Glamorous Department Store.

selfridges.co.uk

Bold, controversial, rude, offensive, insulting and totally insane — but still really funny

South Park, the outrageous adult animated series, first aired in the UK in early 1998 on Sky One and then six months later on Channel 4. It centres around the adventures of four fourth-grade school kids with attitude. One of whom gets killed off in each episode — always in a wickedly cruel accident or due to a disastrous twist of fate to the cry of 'Oh my god, they killed Kenny!' For those not in the know, Cartman is the grouchy couch-potato who, alongside, Stan, Kyle and Kenny, gets himself into all sorts of surreal trouble. So far he's already experienced an 'anal probe' by cow mutilating aliens. So it's no wonder he's sick, twisted and disturbed. They live in the small fictional town of South Park on the border of America with Canada in the Rocky Mountains.

South Park has gained a cult following both in the UK and Stateside. Teenagers, students and young adults alike love its scandalously crass content, amoral overtones and ability to continually shock (and get away with it). South Park certainly isn't suitable for anybody who is easily offended. Its reach isn't confined just to the television, the demand for merchandise exploded.

South Park originated from an animated Christmas card called 'The Spirit of Christmas' which became a cult hit. This led to Trey Parker and Matt Stone being commissioned to produce a half-hour show by Comedy Central – the only all-comedy network at the time that now reaches almost 79 million US cable households. Not only did the series grow from strength to strength but it smashed its own ratings record and won a number of awards including CableACE, Environmental Media and the Nova awards. Even celebrities wanted to get in on the act and George Clooney, Robert Smith and Radiohead to name a few, all became involved.

Alongside the many accolades that South Park has received, merchandise has been a huge success. The four boys Cartman, Kenny, Stan and Kyle made an incredible impact at retail. In the UK alone the South Park brand grew to become worth over £150 million. In fact the UK was the biggest market in the world for videos, soft toys, clothing and condoms. In addition the single 'Chocolate Salty Balls' sung by Chef (Isaac Hayes) reached number one in the UK and spent eleven weeks in the chart.

The release of the movie 'South Park: Bigger Longer and Uncut' created a further frenzy in the media and at retail. Even the soundtrack went platinum and Parker received an Oscar nomination for Best Song.

South Park also made TV history when uttering the word 'shit', a move which undoubtedly served to reinforce its status as one of the coolest cartoon series on TV. Matt and Trey who still write, perform and produce every episode continue to create fresh and hilariously funny material. Despite the absence of parka-clad Kenny, who was finally killed off for good, the fifth season hasn't lost any of its edge – in fact it's funnier.

CHEF
CHOCOLATE SALTY BALLS
INCLUDES FREE COLLECTOR'S SOUTH PARK CHRISTMAS POSTER
PARENTAL GUIDANCE

comedycentral.com

Anyone who happened to be near the Odeon Leicester Square cinema on a certain night in the summer of 1977 could tell that something extraordinary was about to happen. Pre-teens bit their lips, wondering if the film could possibly be as good as they had heard. Inside the cinema, they watched words scroll up a star-filled screen. "A long time ago, in a galaxy far, far away…" The kids sat transfixed as they watched the space epic unfold.

They were watching Star Wars – the film that changed the movies. It confirmed to Hollywood that a movie was much more than just a couple of hours of celluloid – it was a whole 'experience'. Star Wars has broken endless records: it's the highest-grossing film saga (worldwide box office takings were $2.7 billion through Episode I), and it produced the biggest film-based merchandising programme (sales of $7 billion up until Episode II), and the best-selling male action toy and licensed book series ever (the books were translated into over 30 languages).

George Lucas, the film's creator, is an innovator and perfectionist and has continuously pushed the boundaries of filmmaking. Most recently this was demonstrated in Episode II: Attack of The Clones, the first major motion picture to be shot completely digitally and projected digitally in over 100 theatres around the world. To bring his vision to life, Industrial Light & Magic was founded in 1975 to develop new techniques in model making, sound effects and computer graphics. ILM remains a leading visual effects brand, and was involved in virtually every special effects blockbuster of the 1980s and 1990s.

Other Lucas ventures include LucasArts Entertainment Company, an international developer and publisher of interactive entertainment software for PC and home console video game systems. Another is THX – a leader in quality assurance programmes, services and products for the entertainment and consumer electronics industries.

The three original films began with Star Wars (1977) – later subtitled Episode IV: A New Hope – and followed

Engaging, exciting and inspiring audiences with the thrill of continual discovery

with The Empire Strikes Back (1980) and Return of the
Jedi (1983). Vast in scope and rich with original characters
and worlds, the films celebrated heroism and the limitless
potential of the individual.

The break between Return of the Jedi and the beginning
of the second prequel trilogy, Episode I: The Phantom Menace
in 1999, strengthened the original films' classic status, and
allowed a new generation of filmgoers to discover
characters such as C3-PO, R2-D2 and Yoda. To prepare his
audiences for the return of Star Wars, Lucas re-released
the first trilogy in digitally enhanced versions. Then the
website (starwars.com) was enhanced, with magazine stories
about the new film, and special screenings of the trailers
becoming 'events' in themselves.

Episode I was watched by 46% of the potential UK
movie-going population. Episode II: Attack of the Clones was
released in 2002 and developd the legend of Anakin
Skywalker's decent to the Dark Side and eventual
transformation into the Darth Vader of the original trilogy.
Episode III, set to launch in 2005, is now in pre-production.

Lucas says the new trilogy is 'darker and more tragic',
but credible actors such as Ewan McGregor and Samuel
L Jackson add a fresh coolness to the formula of fairy tale
characters, clashing lightsabers and hurtling spacecraft.

Perhaps it's down to the power of The Force, but 25 years
on, Star Wars remains the biggest film franchise in existence.

starwars.com

TAGHeuer

SWISS MADE SINCE 1860

Committed to the pursuit of precision

TAG Heuer has been at the cutting edge of design and technology ever since Edouard Heuer founded the company in Switzerland in 1860. His passionate belief in precision, performance, efficiency and quality is the bedrock of the brand. This has not only become a byword for the ultimate in time-keeping, but also the epitome of style.

TAG Heuer is a legendary brand, worn by legends. Some of the greatest names in motor racing – such as five times world champion in the 1950s, Juan-Manuel Fangio, 1960s hero Jo Siffert and, more recently, the three-times world champion Ayrton Senna – have sworn by TAG Heuer's precision instruments.

The brand has long been recognised as a style leader and is positioned at the top end of market. For example, the Heuer Monaco Chronograph, originally created in 1969, caused a sensation because of its boldly avant-garde design and for featuring the world's first automatic chronograph movement. It became the high-profile model of the era, worn on the wrists of many celebrities, including Steve McQueen, who sported it during the filming of the 1970 film, 'Le Mans'.

The enduring influence on watch design of the Monaco, as well as the 1930s Monza Chronograph and 1960s Carrera, has led TAG Heuer to re-issue the three as modern classics, restating the brand's position at the forefront of aesthetic design and technical innovation for over 140 years.

TAG Heuer's close connections with sport underpin the brand's standing and personality, reinforcing its precision and high performance credentials. TAG Heuer develops its own professional time-keeping equipment for some of the world's most demanding sports disciplines. To take just one example, the brand established its name in motor racing, a field where reliability and precision are paramount, by developing the first ever car-mounted dashboard timing instrument in 1911. In the 1970s TAG Heuer enjoyed the enviable position of official timekeeper for the Scuderia Ferrari Formula One team, and in 2001 celebrated its tenth year as official timekeeper of the FIA Formula One World Championships. For over 50 years, TAG Heuer has also been heavily involved in the worlds of sailing and skiing. Its skiing timekeeping systems, used at the FIS World Ski Championships in 1999 and 2001, are able to measure downhill racers to within 1/1000th of a second. TAG Heuer has also been appointed for 2003 in St Moritz.

TAG Heuer seeks to incorporate this timekeeping technology in the development of its new products,

none more so than in the case of its Professional Sports Watch ranges, the 2000 series (originally introduced in 1982), the Kirium (1997) and the LINK (2000). Indeed in 2001, it launched the Kirium Formula One digital-analog chronograph, combining the ergonomic design of the Kirium range with the ultimate in 1/100th second chronograph technology.

Another core attribute of the brand – elegance in style and design – is also constantly finding expression in new areas. The Alter Ego range is the first TAG Heuer range developed exclusively for women, featuring designs that impressed observers when they were launched in 1999. The company appointed three inspiring women – US Olympic medallist Marion Jones, Spanish actress Ines Sastre and Chinese film star Zhang Ziyi – to act as ambassadors for the range and the TAG Heuer brand as a whole. This continues the long-held tradition of seeking sports heroes and style leaders to showcase and personify all that is best about TAG Heuer and its commitment to design and technology.

tagheuer.com

Four stylish and accessible backdrops for showcasing the best of International and British art from 1500 to 2002

Tate Modern opened in May 2000 with a dramatic nocturnal launch televised by the BBC. London's first national museum for modern art, Tate Modern is housed in the former Bankside Power Station, which was transformed from a defunct industrial space into a stunning gallery.

The former Turbine Hall, running the whole length of the vast building, now makes a breathtaking entrance. At the top of the building is a new two storey glass structure which provides natural light into the upper galleries, and houses a café offering outstanding views across London. Tate Modern's collection covers 1900 to the present day, and includes works by Dalí, Picasso, Matisse, Rothko and Warhol as well as contemporary artists such as Dorothy Cross, Gilbert & George and Susan Hiller.

From the day it opened (and even before, in fact) Tate Modern has been a talking point. During its opening week it occupied 317 inches of column space in the national press, making it the fifth biggest story that week. And in its first year, Tate Modern attracted 5.25 million visitors, with over a million visiting in the first six weeks alone. Tate Britain focuses on British art and is housed in Tate's original 19th century building a few miles further west along the

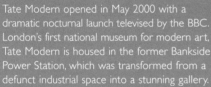

Dame Barbara Hepworth's Sea Form (Porthmeor) 1958
© Alan Bowness, Hepworth Estate

© Tate Photography

Thames at Millbank. The Collection presents an unrivalled picture of the development of art in Britain from 1500 to the present day. Renaming and redefining the 'original Tate', against the backdrop of Tate Modern's precocious success, was an interesting strategic challenge for any brand. But by September 2001 Wallpaper* magazine was not alone in seeing Tate Britain writ large on the cultural radar when it told its readers "Leave Tate Modern to the tourist hordes: this one's for the connoisseur".

The Tate's out-of-London galleries in Liverpool and St Ives (Cornwall) opened in 1988 and 1993 respectively. Tate Liverpool is located in a converted warehouse in the city's Albert Dock, whilst Tate St Ives makes the most of the legendary Cornish coastal light with its beachfront position. Both present art selected from the Tate Collection and special exhibitions of contemporary art loaned from other public and private collections.

It was the splitting of the London Tate Gallery into two that stimulated the creation of a new identity. In March 2000 a new logo, a Tate font and a colour palette symbolising openness, change and vision were unveiled. There was also a newly designed website, uniforms designed by Paul Smith, and signage.

The launch of Tate Modern and Tate Britain was accompanied by a high-impact advertising campaign which communicated the spirit and values of the new Tate through adverts which used the strapline 'Look Again, Think Again'. As well as collaborating with The Guardian (the media partner for the launch of both galleries, and a key collaborator today), Tate Modern's marketing campaign involved six million branded coffee cups in Coffee Republic cafes, Wagamama chopsticks promoting the Tate Membership scheme, an in-store concession at Selfridges, Tate Beer produced in conjunction with Oliver Peyton's Mash restaurant, and a special Royal Mail stamp.

Research has shown that international awareness of both Tate Modern and Tate Britain has continued to rise, with a growth of 18% between 2000 and 2001. In addition, Tate Modern became on launch the most popular modern art gallery in the world, as well as the third most popular tourist attraction in Britain.

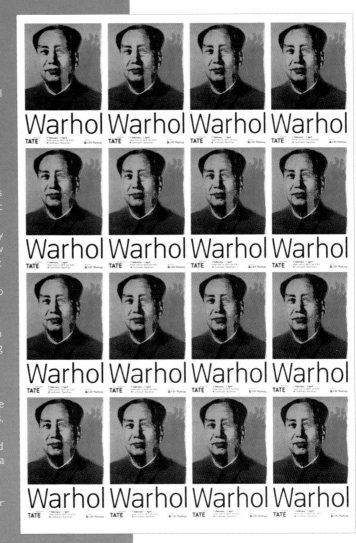

tate.org.uk

the healing garden

Holistic fragrances for the well-being of mind, body and spirit

The frantic pace of life in the 21st century means that people are increasingly concerned about their physical and emotional health and are looking for natural, holistic ways to enhance their everyday lives.

Music can soothe or uplift, certain colours can induce a calmer frame of mind but scents have the most powerful impact on our feelings. Smells are associated with memory and are connected to the emotional centres of the brain.

Coty, the largest creator of mass-market fragrances in the world, recognised early on that people were beginning to use fragrances in a new way, to help them feel refreshed, relaxed and healthy. The company also noticed the growing trend towards self-pampering and the demand for natural products.

In 1997, Coty started to look at the power of aromacology, an emerging discipline which lies on the boundary between science and nature and which is dedicated to exploring the ways in which fragrances affect our feelings and moods and can improve our quality of life.

As a result, Coty launched The Healing Garden, which is based on the science of aromacology and harnesses the power of plants to promote a sense of well-being, both inside and out. The Healing Garden uses botanical extracts in all its five ranges: Lavender for relaxation, Gingerlily for positivity, Green Tea for harmony, Jasmine for sensuality and ZZZ…sleep easy for a good night's sleep. Each fragrance comes in a number of formulations — eau de toilette, body spray, bath and shower gel, body lotion, bath soak and in some cases, scented candles to further enhance the brand experience. Subtle, calming, uncluttered packaging with tactile textures are used with mute rainbow colours reflecting the scents. Consumers are encouraged to experiment with the various fragrances and use them according to their mood. Lavender helps to relax and work away stress. Ginger Lily with St John's Wort extract is a refreshing pick-me-up to help awaken optimism and energy. Green Tea helps restore balance and harmony to mind, body and spirit. Jasmine inspires a sense of feminine fulfilment and sensuality. The Healing Garden also addresses sleeplessness — one of the biggest problems of modern life as more and more people find it hard to switch off from the stresses of the day. The ZZZ…sleep easy range is designed to help repair frazzled nerves, soothe the senses and help lure the body into a restful slumber using natural botanical extracts of chamomile, vanilla bean and orange blossom.

The Healing Garden's advertising, consists mainly of print work and reflects the brands values in its uncluttered and calming approach.

In the UK, The Healing Garden has teamed up with the Lavender Trust, a cancer charity that raises funds to provide services for younger women with breast cancer. Five pence from the sale of each Lavender product from The Healing Garden is donated to the charity, evidence of the company's commitment to socially responsible programmes. There is, of course, also a complementary fit between the charity's name and one of The Healing Garden's essential ingredients.

In the past, aromatherapy and aromacology products were a very niche market, aimed at consumers with a particular interest in alternative therapies. The Healing Garden, in contrast, is a worldwide brand that is relevant to a much broader spectrum of consumers. It is now a crucial part of Coty's strategy to develop new markets and build a category it has identified as the non-traditional fragrance experience.

coty.com

Socially irreverent, fun, intelligent, satirical, fresh and topical

The Simpsons was created by Matt Groening and debuted in the late 1980s as a series of shorts that went on to receive worldwide acclaim when launched as a full-length animated sitcom in December 1989. Thirteen TV series later, The Simpsons is not only the longest running animated TV series ever, it is also a cultural phenomenon and, according to many fans, the best TV programme in existence. Homer Simpson was voted number one in Channel 4's poll of the '100 Greatest TV Characters of All Time'. The Simpsons was also placed number one in the same station's vote for the '100 Greatest Kids' Shows of All Time'.

Few people in the UK could fail to be familiar with the Simpson family and Homer and Marge's struggle to bring up Bart, Lisa and Maggie. Indeed, their catch phrases are almost part of the language with 'D'oh!' often being heard when things don't go as planned. The Simpsons live in Evergreen Terrace, the nicest lower-middle class section of the fictional US town of Springfield. Homer is a safety inspector at the town's nuclear power plant, but often forgets his job to follow his dreams, although his great plans never quite work out as he intends. Other residents of Springfield include the Flanders, the Simpsons' law abiding, do-gooding neighbours; Moe, who owns a run down local bar; Krusty the Clown, a dubious kids' entertainer; and Mr Burns, Homer's boss and owner of the power plant. The Simpsons has had many guest appearances from fans of the show over the years, including Aerosmith, Tom Jones, Bette Midler, Britney Spears and Blink-182 who have had cameo roles in the programme.

The Simpsons licensing programme has existed since the early 1990s and has been developed and maintained in close partnership with Gracie Films and the creators of the TV series. The Simpsons has a strong and innovative presence at retail around the world, with a wealth of products in categories as diverse as gifts, clothing, food, toys and games, accessories, videos and video games, books and collectibles.

In the UK, The Simpsons continues to be one of the most successful character licences on the market and appeals to both children and adults. As with the show itself, it appeals on several levels. Its success is also due to the calibre of licensees who are carefully monitored to ensure that every product represents The Simpsons in all its idiosyncratic and irreverent glory, accurately reflecting the TV show and so delighting consumers.

The Simpsons merchandise has developed and grown over the course of time to match changing consumer trends and seasonal events, with new products in areas such as snowboarding, football and Halloween.

With regards to food and promotions The Simpsons have, over the years, linked up with top-tier brands in the UK, including Burger King (Kids' Meals), Nestlé (Kit Kat), Ferrero (Nutella), Kraft (Lunchables) and Kellogg's (Bart Simpsons No ProblemOs cereal). Tailor-made promotional activities around retail windows such as Father's Day (Clintons) and Back to School (Marks & Spencer) have also been introduced.

The best advertisement for The Simpsons is naturally its unsurpassed TV presence on both Sky One and BBC2 with Channel 4 soon to follow. Indeed The Simpsons has guaranteed TV broadcasting until 2010. Aye carumba!

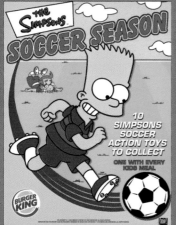

thesimpsons.com

MATT GROENING

Cities are cultural and stylistic melting pots – they are where new trends, movements and fashions are formed. Without urban life, the world would be a very dull and colourless place. And without Time Out, urban life in many of the world's greatest cities wouldn't be so vibrant.

Since its foundation in 1968, Time Out has become a byword in guides to city living. The business that was started by a student, Tony Elliott, with a £75 gift from his aunt, has become a publishing powerhouse. The most comprehensive arts and entertainment listings magazine in London sold 5,000 copies when it was first launched as a single-sheet poster in 1968 and now boasts a weekly circulation of nearly 87,000.

Over the years, Time Out has come to represent the energy and diversity of London. Its independent listings and in-depth features cover the culture of the capital in all its guises; be it dance, the gay scene, books, sport, events for students, clubs and bars, theatre, art, comedy or film. Its expert reviews are fiercely impartial, written by people with a genuine passion for their field and who are as outspoken about what they love and hate as the thousands of loyal readers who regard Time Out as 'London's voice'. Time Out is not afraid of voicing its opinion, even if some of its readers don't always agree.

Under the guidance of Tony Elliott (who still runs the company) Time Out has expanded into new areas. Most notably, Time Out's reach has stretched beyond its spiritual home of London, with Time Out City Guides (published by Penguin) now covering 35 cities and regions around the world. In 2002, new titles include guides to Andalucia, Toronto, Bangkok and Stockholm.

Time Out is now also published weekly in that other style-leading metropolis – New York – and a portfolio of monthly licensed titles are published in Abu Dhabi, Cyprus, Dubai and Istanbul.

The leading listings bible with the latest news, honest views and knowledgeable insights

The individualistic and authoritative Time Out voice has been applied to other guides for London, such as the Student Guide, the Visitors' Guide and the Shopping Guide. If you're looking for the latest 'in' places to eat and drink, the Time Out Eating & Drinking and the Pubs & Bars Guides are essential reading. Similar gastronomic bibles are produced for Paris and New York.

All this diversity goes to prove that when it comes to having a finger on the pulse of city life and having a brand which people respect, Time Out has an unbeatable reputation. It doesn't own restaurants, but its annual Eating Awards are London's most prestigious. It doesn't make films but, via the Time Out Arts Trust, it is a keen supporter of London Arts. And, it doesn't own theatres or comedy clubs but its annual Live Awards recognise the best new talent around.

Time Out is one of those brands that has earned its iconic status by doing a simple job and doing it brilliantly and consistently well. For nearly 35 years, Time Out has stuck to its mandate of providing information: clearly, simply, comprehensively and without fear or favour.

timeout.com

'IT MAKES ME FEEL LIKE A PART OF THE CITY.' TO

TOMMY ▬ HILFIGER

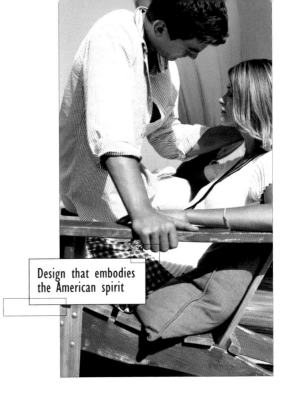

Tommy Hilfiger says his brand is dedicated to living the spirit of the American dream; he believes in the spirit of youth and draws on this feeling for inspiration. His guiding principle is that his clothes are designed for anyone with a young attitude to life – embracing infants to 80 year olds.

Tommy Hilfiger began his career in 1969 when he used his life savings of $150 to buy a job lot of trendy bell-bottom jeans in New York and drive them to his rural home town. He began selling the jeans to local teenagers. Armed with an understanding of what consumers wanted, he opened his own store, People's Place, and by the age of 26 had used the profits to open ten stores in the US. Self taught, he then began designing clothes that his customers wanted but could not find.

Design that embodies the American spirit

In 1979, Hilfiger moved to New York to pursue a career as a fashion designer. His first signature collection was introduced in 1985 and was supported with a bold advertising campaign that declared Hilfiger to be the new leader in men's fashion.

His range of classic American clothing with a twist – the 'preppy' look, often in shades of red, white and blue, wittily enhanced with his signature contrast linings and coloured stitching on button holes – became an instant success.

In 1996, Tommy Hilfiger launched the brand in Europe with his men's sportswear collection and Tommy and Tommy Girl fragrances. He held a high profile fashion show at London Fashion Week and also sponsored Ferrari – a complementary, aspirational brand. Now the main thrust of Tommy Hilfiger's promotional campaigns revolve around advertising in print and outdoor media, with ads reflecting the fresh, youthful attitude of the brand. Other UK promotional activity includes advertising in print media and outdoor on London taxis and Manchester's trams.

In the UK Tommy Hilfiger can be found in stores such as Harrods, Selfridges and Harvey Nichols as well as through the Tommy Hilfiger store on London's Sloane Street and a recently launched store in Manchester's King Street. The Tommy Hilfiger brand is also sold around the world including Central and South America and the Far East.

The product range includes casual clothing for men and women, tailored clothing for men, kids collections, fragrances, make-up, eyewear, footwear and accessories. In autumn 2002 the brand will be further expanded through the launch of the Hilfiger watch collection.

Tommy Hilfiger's philosophy is based on creating a true mixture of sportswear and tailored clothing. As he says himself, "I take sportswear and tailored clothing – the foundations of our collection – and put them in a blender to create something new and exciting."

Tommy Hilfiger's designs have been worn by everybody from Kate Winslet and Eddie Irvine to Lauren Bush. His long association with the music industry has led to Hilfiger logos appearing on stage, album covers and in party photos snapped by the paparazzi. Having previously sponsored artists such as Lenny Kravitz and the Rolling Stones, Hilfiger now takes a more relaxed approach to celebrity endorsement. He is currently using a core group of inspirational brand ambassadors throughout the UK, who all consistently wear his clothes.

Tommy Hilfiger now has plans for a store expansion programme in Europe, with stand-alone outlets due to launch in major European cities over the next year.

TOMMY ■ HILFIGER

tommy.com

TOPSHOP

A transformed fashion brand which has got the fashion world buzzing

Topshop has undergone an amazing transformation since the mid 1990s, changing from a cheap and cheerful outfitter for the nation's teenagers into a seriously cool, trend-setting label. Topshop is still good value and accessible but the difference is that its designs are no longer confined to the school disco. They are also worn by the likes of Madonna, Destiny's Child and Kate Moss, all of whom are customers at Topshop's giant flagship store in London's Oxford Street. And this truly is a fashion lover's mecca. The largest fashion store in the world, it boasts retro fashion, designer collections, metres and metres of high fashion, an accessories floor, a footwear department and, throughout, a vibrant atmosphere created by an in-store radio station, fashion shows and TV walls on each floor.

Style bibles agree that Topshop is the name of the moment. Vogue's staff regularly drop in to see what's new and have even declared that 'Topshop is a favourite among the fashion pack'. The Times has said that 'it's now a fashion faux-pas not to go there'. The Sunday Times has enthused that 'the high street has never looked so haute, and it's all down to Topshop'.

Topshop's ability to sell credible design at high street prices is one of the brand's major achievements. Furthermore, its success lies in being able to translate new styles and trends quickly whilst making them affordable to the fashion savvy consumer.

Some 180,000 shoppers visit the Oxford Street store every week, drawn by this reputation for not only keeping up with, but staying ahead of, the latest trends. This has been proven in recent seasons where its collections have actually been shown before the catwalk. Staying ahead means moving fast and Topshop can put up to 300 new lines on sale in just one week.

The TS Design initiative exemplifies how Topshop has become the high street darling of the fashion world. Since 1998, Topshop has provided financial support for young designers by sponsoring their shows in return for exclusive limited edition collections. Some of the names who have worked with the retailer, such as Clements Ribeiro, Tracey Boyd and Hussein Chalayan, are now successful labels in their own right. Topshop is currently working with some of the industry's leading creative talent, such as Sophia Kokosalaki and Marcus Lupfer to design for its TS Design label.

While many other retailers belatedly copy the latest look, Topshop's crack team frequently sets the agenda. The designs featured in its Unique range – a new home-grown hip label – show this in action; the fashions created by Topshop's own designers have been extremely well received. As The Face recently wrote: 'Topshop does not merely ape the catwalk – it is a dream factory that initiates and innovates, and creates its own fashion'.

Topshop's commitment to supporting new fashion talent is further reflected in its sponsorship of London Fashion Week's New Generation Award, which has launched the careers of 'fashion royalty' like Stella McCartney and Alexander McQueen. Topshop also supports the Prince's Trust Graduate Fashion Week, the biggest student fashion event and an important showcase for grass-roots talent.

This support plays a major role in keeping the British fashion industry's creative juices flowing, as well as affirming Topshop's new-found position at fashion's top table. This status is also reflected in the way in which Topshop advertises. Print is the brand's preferred medium, and outdoor advertisements are used in conjunction with ads in the most stylish of magazines where Topshop's sassy, sexy and chic clothing and accessories sit comfortably alongside designer labels.

topshop.co.uk

vιrgιn atlantιc

Distinctive, fun-loving, innovative and continually offering a high level of luxury

Launched in 1984, Virgin Atlantic started life as an eccentricity – an unexpected offshoot of Richard Branson's mainly music-based Virgin Group. The ebullient entrepreneur launched the airline in just three months, finding an aircraft, designing uniforms and then setting off on an inaugural flight to New York with a planeload of friends, celebrities and media.

The giants of the industry didn't rate the cheeky newcomer's chances of success very highly. Little did they know that Virgin Atlantic would eventually become Britain's second largest long haul carrier and the third largest European carrier across the North Atlantic. Customers flocked to the new airline that didn't treat them as if they were on a conveyor belt and combined good service and value with a sense of style and fun. Everything about its attitude was quintessentially Virgin: the small newcomer taking on the complacent and established giants; the people's champion, offering lower fares and better service whilst maintaining quality and innovative product developments.

The airline industry was affected more than most by the tragic events of September 11th 2001. There was an immediate and significant reduction in passengers, and a number of airlines suffered bankruptcy. The industry is slowly rebuilding passenger confidence but it will be some time before the long-term consequences are fully apparent. It is clear that in order to survive and compete in this challenging environment it is vital for airlines to adapt and evolve an ever-improving range of services.

Even though it has now grown up, Virgin Atlantic still retains a distinctive sense of style which sets it apart from its rivals. Its Upper Class service has set new standards of comfort and innovation, winning every major award in the travel industry since 1984. Whether it's travelling to the airport in a chauffer-driven limousine or even a 'LimoBike', relaxing in one of the airline's award-winning lounges, getting a head and neck massage from an in-flight beauty therapist, or sleeping in all 6'8" of the airline's revolutionary sleeper seat, Virgin passengers travel in style.

The same goes for economy and premium economy, which also challenge the norms of air travel, with levels of comfort and service not offered by other airlines. On-board entertainment has always been Virgin Atlantic's forte. It was the first airline to offer business class passengers individual TVs, back in 1989, and the first to provide personal TV screens offering a choice of channels to passengers in all classes, in 1991. In the near future, Virgin Atlantic will continue pushing the boundaries of in-flight entertainment, offering passengers internet access, email, video and audio on demand.

The greatest and best known advertisement for Virgin is Richard Branson himself. Often perceived as the 'consumer hero', Virgin's brand values reflect his own personality. At one and the same time Branson is one of the UK's most admired businessmen, and one of the most flamboyant. His daredevil antics, such as ballooning across the Atlantic, have given the Virgin brand extra publicity.

The airline's TV advertisements, featuring icons like Helen Mirren, Anna Friel, Iggy Pop and even Miss Piggy, accentuate the message that Virgin Atlantic is anything but 'just another airline'. Like these brand ambassadors, Virgin Atlantic owes its success to challenging the status quo, dictating rather than following fashion, and constantly reinventing its image to stay fresh in consumers' minds.

Miss Piggy in the Back Seat

virgin.com/atlantic

vitra.

Vitra is renowned for turning the workspace into a productive, motivating and appealing place to be and prides itself on working with major designers throughout the world, including Philippe Starck, Antonio Citterio, Ron Arad and Norman Foster. Vitra furniture – chairs, desks, seating units, room dividers, stools and furnishing systems – can be seen almost everywhere in the modern world, from the headquarters of multi-national companies to airport terminals and TV studios, as well as in many homes.

With an ongoing policy of using eco-friendly materials and techniques, the furniture includes only a small number of components, is sturdy yet light, and recyclable once it reaches the

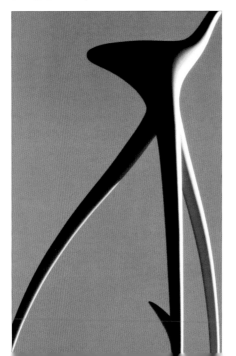

end of its long life-span. Designs are technologically outstanding, beautiful in their simplicity, ergonomic and built to last.

The company was founded in Switzerland but manufacturing started – and continues – in Weil am Rhein, just over the border in Germany. In the 1950s, Vitra won the rights to produce the designs by Charles & Ray Eames and George Nelson in Europe. Such is the timeless appeal of these creations from the 1950s and 1960s that they are still being manufactured today.

In the late 1970s, ergonomic principles were introduced in the quest for the ideal chair that supports good posture, invites movement and is pleasing to the eye. The Vitramat revolutionised office seating with its patented synchronised movement. Not losing sight of being at the cutting edge of design, in the mid 1980s Vitra began putting new ideas to the test by co-operating with leading international exponents of the avant-garde. They also acquired the European and Middle Eastern rights to Eames and Nelson products, resulting in a further production facility being built, designed by architect Nicholas Grimshaw.

After a major factory fire in Weil am Rhein, Rolf Fehlbaum, CEO of Vitra, turned disaster into opportunity and commissioned emerging architects throughout the late 1980s and 1990s to produce an architectural park. This includes the Vitra fire station by Zaha Hadid, conference pavilion by Tadao Ando, a production facility by Alvaro Siza, and the Vitra Design Museum by Frank Gehry. This unique centre presents temporary exhibitions on furniture design and houses one of the world's largest collections of contemporary chairs.

The new era also brought an ecological awareness to meet growing demand, and an internal ecology committee was set up to discuss environmental topics.

The 1990s also bestowed the brand with a cluster of awards, including the Swiss Design Prize 1991, Corporate Design Award 1994, European Community Design Prize 1994 and German Prize for Communications Design 1998. Countless Vitra products have also won international awards.

Today, the company employs 1090 staff worldwide including its headquarters in Birsfelden, near Basle, Switzerland. There are production locations in Germany, Switzerland and the US, and showrooms all over the world.

Vitra designs are featured regularly in American, British, French, German and Swiss TV programmes and can be seen at the permanent design exhibition at the Museum of Modern Art in New York. Vitra also has many supporters amongst international businesses – Mercedes-Benz, Lufthansa, Apple and Coca-Cola all use Vitra furniture in their workspaces. Vitra can also be found in Moscow and Dubai airport terminals as well as in the Eurostar terminal at Waterloo, London.

Vitra is recognised by those who look for timeless style, comfortable and ergonomic design with an eco-friendly attitude to furniture selection.

vitra.com

Vivienne Westwood

Rebellious, adventurous, outrageous and a teasing epitome of British eccentricity

Famous for her innovative, inspiring and quirky designs, Vivienne Westwood has become a true fashion icon. Vivienne Isabel Swire, aka Vivienne Westwood, the daughter of a cobbler and a cotton mill worker was born in Derbyshire in 1941. She began designing in 1971 after meeting entrepreneur Malcolm McLaren, best know for managing the Sex Pistols. By this time she was living in London, had been a primary school teacher and had been married and divorced. For over a decade Westwood and McLaren ran a shop called 'Let It Rock' on the King's Road which showcased their radical designs. Westwood rapidly became one of the leading inspirations of punk fashion and was even dubbed the 'Queen of Punk'.

The shop also sold Rock n' Roll records, which was unusual at this time as this kind of music was not broadcast on British radio and hippies were still in fashion. The shop was reinvented several times as Westwood's ideas evolved. It was renamed and the interior redesigned first as 'Too Fast To Live, Too Young To Die' and stocked clothing for Rockers. By 1974 the shop was called 'Sex' and emphasized themes of bondage, sadomasochism, and body fetishes. In 1977 it was renamed again 'Seditionaries' and then 'The World's End' in the 1980s; a name which it still retains. It now stocks Westwood's Anglomania collection and accessories, while the building's backward spinning clock is a renowned tourist attraction.

In the early 1980s, Westwood began showing in Paris; the first British designer to do so since Mary Quant. Collections such as Pirates (1981-82), Savages (1982), Buffalo Girls (1982-83), Punkature (1983), and Witches (1983) helped to create the 'New Romantic' look which penetrated throughout popular culture. By the end of the decade, John Fairchild, editor of fashion bible, Women's Wear Daily, had hailed Vivienne Westwood one of the six best designers in the world in his book 'Chic Savages.'

The 1990s kicked off with Westwood being named British Fashion Designer of the Year by the British Fashion Council, while ITV's flagship arts programme, The South Bank Show, aired a one-hour profile of her.

Traditional British fabrics have remained greatly important to Westwood: Harris Tweed, Scottish Tartans, Irish Linens and wools are modified to the designer's specifications, while specially designed tartans are woven for her, such as her own 'MacAndreas' tartan. This was designed for the Anglomania collection and named after Westwood's designer husband Andreas Kronthaler. This is now displayed together with time-honoured, traditional tartans in the Lochcarron Museum of Tartan in Scotland – an incredible achievement for a designer to be accepted in this way.

Vivienne Westwood has amassed a string of other accolades including the Queen's Award for Export (1998)

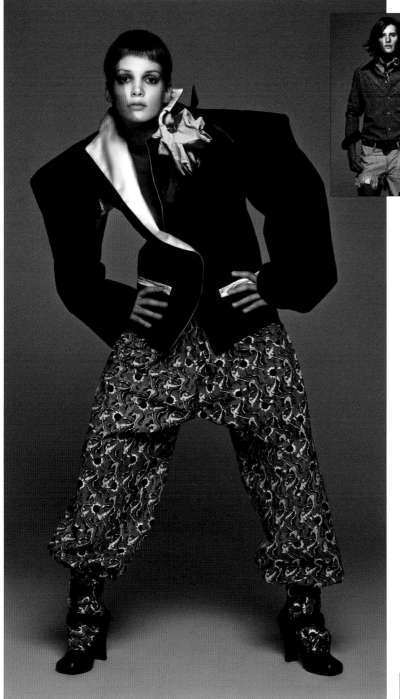

in recognition of the company's growing export market. In 1992, Westwood became an Honorary Senior Fellow of the Royal College of Art and, following her listing in the Birthday Honours issued by Buckingham Palace, was presented with an OBE. In addition, Vivienne Westwood is the first designer to be honoured at the Moët & Chandon Fashion Tribute. This prestigious annual event, held in conjunction with the Victoria & Albert Museum, honours leading lights from the world of fashion, whose creativity and vision has had a profound influence on our lifestyle.

The Vivienne Westwood brand now consists of four labels: Vivienne Westwood Gold Label sold in Westwood's Mayfair store; Red Label which is the diffusion line; MAN which, as one would expect, is the male collection and finally ANGLOMANIA, the designer's casualwear line. Vivienne Westwood's personality is reflected in all the collections and continues to challenge expectations.

vivennewestwood.com

New Beetle - youthful, charismatic, colourful, outgoing, fun loving, entertaining, quirky and individualistic

While it rekindles the magic of its legendary namesake, the new Beetle is not a mere update of the original but a completely new and modern — almost futuristic — car. It carries no name on its body but it is unmistakably a Volkswagen Beetle and is recognised with affection by young and old alike.

The Beetle's smooth lines and geometric arches are simultaneously thoroughly modern and evocative of its long and distinguished heritage. For example, a single round instrument displays the speed, rev counter, engine temperature and fuel gauge, but all the displays are illuminated by a glowing indigo blue light against which the needles stand out in vibrant red. As a playful reflection of the past, there are loop shaped grab handles above the passenger and rear seats and webbed storage compartments in the doors.

Available in eleven colours, including metallic and pearlised finishes, the new Beetle is eye-catching and head turning. The interior is creatively sculpted from high quality textured plastics and textiles, with a bright finish on the steering wheel, gear lever and hand brake — plus a flower vase, complete with a gerbera, on the dashboard.

But the Beetle is far more than just a ray of sunny individuality: it offers all the creature comforts and state-of-the-art safety, security and performance features you would expect from a product in the Volkswagen range.

The new Beetle is much bigger than the original, both inside and out, and shares no parts with its predecessor. Based on Volkswagen's current Golf chassis, its engine is in the front, and it is a front-wheel drive. It is available with a choice of five different engines, including two high-performance versions and a V5 Sport Edition. When the 'Concept 1' Beetle was unveiled at the Geneva Motor Show in 1996, it provoked a huge response, with Beetle enthusiasts worldwide logging on to the Volkswagen website to register their interest. Two years later the car was launched at the Detroit Motor Show and a year later won the prestigious North American Car of the Year award. It went on sale in mainland Europe in November 1998. Demand from the UK was so high that 900 left-hand drive versions were imported to help assuage demand until the right-hand drive version became available in January 2000.

Even before the new Beetle came on to the market, enthusiastic media attention ensured that 90% of people knew of its existence. But since the main talking point was its appearance, the launch was designed to convey its strong technical credentials in addition to its appearance through the 'Fun on the outside, serious underneath' campaign.

True to the original classic, the new Beetle's design appeal is classless, appealing to a wider cross section of people than most other cars, those who fondly recall the past as well as young people who have no connection to the original. But whereas the original Beetle provided basic transportation, the new Beetle is an upmarket lifestyle vehicle. It's highly emotional; a car that makes the experience of driving fun again.

volkswagen.co.uk

wagamama

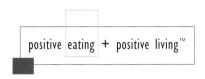

positive eating + positive living™

www.wagamama.com

london . dublin . amsterdam

Japanese style and design is all the rage at the moment, influencing many areas of Western culture, including fashion, animation, consumer electronics and food. The latter area has felt a particularly strong influence from Japan, as the growing penchant for noodle bars and sushi shows.

The thing trendy urbanites love about Japanese food is its freshness, healthiness and the chic minimalist design of the restaurants. However, one restaurant chain has managed to be a step (or two) ahead of the trend: Wagamama has been working on this philosophy and has regular queues outside its doors week after week since it opened its first noodle bar in London in 1992.

The essence of Wagamama is a no-nonsense combination: simple, high quality yet inexpensive food served up in a sleek, minimalist canteen-style setting, with bench seats and no reservations

alongside an open-plan kitchen. Together these all contribute to the noisy, vibrant, buzz of the restaurants. This carefully balanced formula was an instant hit when the first restaurant opened on Streatham Street, near the British Museum in London's Bloomsbury district. Thirteen additional Wagamama restaurants have since opened in London, and the brand has also expanded nationally, opening in Manchester and Nottingham, with branches planned for Bristol and St Albans. In addition, the first Wagamama branch outside the UK opened in Dublin in 1998, Amsterdam followed in 2000 and May 2002 saw Wagamama going down under with the opening of a restaurant in Sydney. With more international branches in the pipeline, Wagamama is simply following its customers' demands.

Much can be learned about Wagamama by examining the meaning of the name itself. Translated literally from Japanese, wagamama means 'wilful/selfish child'. But a broader interpretation would explain the selfishness in terms of looking after oneself, in terms of positive eating and positive living. A single-minded belief in the strength of its own formula, and letting the quality of its product speak for itself, has built Wagamama into an extremely strong and much admired brand, as well as enhancing its cool credentials.

The personality of Wagamama is also very apparent in its uncomplicated advertising. An image that is frequently used in its ads, amongst other communications, is that of an eager diner with a large bowl completely covering her face as she slurps up what is left in the bottom. Shot in black and white, the image gives an air of being both innocent and childlike but confident and wilful at the same time.

At the prestigious Retailers' Retailer of the Year Awards 2002, which are organised by Martin Information, one of the sector's leading business information providers, Wagamama's simple successful formula was voted 'Best Concept' and it was a finalist in the 'Best Design' category.

Wagamama's singular approach is reflected in its unconventional way of doing things – it doesn't get carried away with some of the fuss and ceremony often found in restaurants and focuses on delivering great food at excellent value (average spend is around £12 per head). Orders are taken on the latest technically advanced hand-held electronic devices and zapped straight to the kitchen, where each dish is cooked and served immediately. If that means a party of people getting their food at different times, then so be it. Whether it's sitting at a bench next to a stranger, queuing until seats become free, or getting your food before or after your friends, enjoying Wagamama is all about going with the flow.

In fact, its approach, environment and ethos are as fresh as the food itself.

www.wagamama.com
london dublin amsterdam

www.wagamama.com
london dublin amsterdam

wagamama.com

It all started in January 2001, when Microsoft unveiled the most powerful gaming system ever built – the Xbox. Its sole purpose? To provide the best video game experience available.

The industry watched with interest as Microsoft's entry into the video games market promised to be the biggest shake-up since Sony launched Playstation in 1995. In addition to having online gaming capabilities, Xbox can also play DVD movies and CDs. It has more than three times the graphics performance of the latest generation of game consoles as well as advanced audio power. Xbox gives game designers the technology to realise their vision of great games that are challenging, exhilarating and fun. For example, enemies are more intelligent and learn how you are playing the game, which gives a more realistic feel to the game play.

Xbox's built in hard drive further increases the quality of graphics as well as the overall

speed of games. These factors combined create an experience closer to virtual reality than ever before, allowing players to become truly immersed in the gaming experience, bluring the edges between fantasy and reality.

Xbox proved to be one of the most successful video game console launches ever, selling 1.5 million systems in the US in the weeks between its launch in November 2001 and the end of December that year. Xbox was launched in Europe on March 14th 2002 amidst green light shows, celebratory events and long queues of gamers waiting to get their hands on the future of gaming.

In the run up to the UK launch, Xbox ran a competition with the virtual '2-D' band, Gorrilaz. In addition, Xbox 'sampling pods' were set up at snowboarding shows, record shops and music awards as well as at the openings of stylish new bars. This gave the young, trendy games enthusiasts an early tantalising taste of what the brand was about. Furthermore a series of 'Xperience' events were held around the UK. Especially constructed gaming zones were

designed to create the right environment of excitement, escape and futuristic adventure, where gamers could put the Xbox and some of its exclusive games such as Halo and Project Gotham Racing through their paces. Halo has the much sought after accolade of being one of only a handful of games ever to garner a ten out of ten score in Edge, the influential European games magazine.

Xbox's streetwise credibility was further enhanced with the use of guerrilla and viral marketing to get people talking about the brand in the run up to its launch. Tying in with the brand's core message – 'Play More' – this included drawing hopscotch squares onto city pavements. The 'X' logo was also drawn in chalk around city centres, giving it a 'graffiti art' kudos.

The internet also played an important part in getting people talking about Xbox. A short film, depicting a person's journey from birth to death in three hair-raising minutes, was 'seeded' on the web so that people would pass it on. Such was the success of the film, which ends with the line 'Life is Short. Play More', that it was made into a cinema and TV commercial.

A total of twenty games were available on the day of launch with around 60 titles available by the end of June 2002. Many more are in development from some of the world's best game publishers and developers, including Electronic Arts, Infogrames, Sega, Codemasters, Eidos, UbiSoft, Activision and Konami.

As a philosophy on life, 'Play More' has much to recommend it. And, like life itself, Xbox is more than just a game.

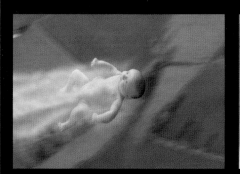

xbox.com/uk

SUSHI

With its conveyor belts, robots and beer on tap YO! is a bit cheeky and not scared of breaking new ground

Before YO! Sushi launched in 1997, Japanese food was expensive, elitist and hard to come by in the UK. Simon Woodroffe, founder of the brand, changed all that.

YO! Sushi was built on a throw away remark made by a Japanese friend of Woodroffe's who suggested that he open a conveyor belt sushi bar with girls in PVC miniskirts. Woodroffe, a former set designer for rock bands, readily confesses that he knew nothing about running restaurants and nothing about sushi other than the fact that he liked it, but the idea stuck. The PVC miniskirts never made it into the finished concept but the conveyor belt, robotic drinks trolleys, colour coded pricing system, beer on tap and self heating plates did.

In Japan, conveyor belt restaurants are basic and functional – the equivalent of a British greasy spoon café, but Woodroffe decided to take the concept up market and sell not just sushi but

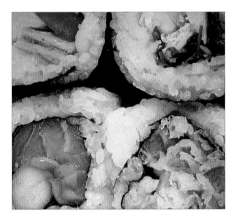

a lifestyle too. So the YO! brand stands for integrity, truthfulness, and good value and aims to be an exhilarating exclamation of life and celebrates optimism for the future.

YO! has successfully tapped into a growing fascination for all things Japanese and above all, has given eating out a sense of fun. Why wave at a waitress for attention when you can press a call button? Why have to wait for a drink when you can serve yourself? In the early days many customers weren't familiar with sushi, but they were tempted into the restaurants by the gadgetry, tried the sushi and liked it.

From its first outlet in London's Soho the YO! empire has grown and grown. There are now fifteen YO! Sushi restaurants and bars across London and in Edinburgh with a restaurant planned for Manchester. The first international branch will opened in Kuwait and plans to take the YO! experience to the US are also underway.

YO! Sushi have introduced raw fish to a mass audience selling YO! branded boxes of sushi in Sainsbury's and Safeway. And for non raw fish eaters there are many hot fish and meat dishes as well as vegetarian alternatives. Event catering through YO! to GO delivers portable conveyor belts, sushi, hot food, robots, drinks and a general sense of YO!ness to parties and functions.

The brand has also expanded into YO! Below – technologically advanced bars which feature sunken tables, smoke extracting ash trays, tarot readings, massages, singing bar staff and self serve beer which is metered.

The YO! Sushi team are fearless and are prepared to push the boundaries of conventional thinking. Innovation is key to the brand's

success and YO! does not rely on focus groups or endless market research but on gut instinct. For example, YO! Sushi ventures where more conventional restaurants fear to tread. The team recently installed, with much success, a conveyor belt at Paddington Station serving both office workers and travellers and is currently looking to open at Heathrow Airport by the end of 2002.

The YO! brand is also developing in new areas to further build upon its international retail brand credentials. A hotel concept is set to launch this year as a low cost, city centre alternative to stuffy hotel chains. Body YO! a Japanese-style health spa is also under consideration as well as a YO! Japan fashion range. All of which will, no doubt continue to reflect Woodroffe's renowned ability to challenge convention.

yosushi.com

adidas
adidas UK Ltd
PO Box 39
Pepper Road
Hazel Grove
Stockport
Cheshire
SK7 5SD

Agent Provocateur
Agent Provocateur
16 Pont Street
London
SW1X 9EN

Alexander McQueen
Alexander McQueen
10 Amwell Street
London
EC1R 1UQ

Apple
Apple
2 Furzeground Way
Stockley Park
Uxbridge
Middlesex
UB11 1BB

Asahi
Asahi Beer Europe Ltd
17 Connaught Place
London
W2 2EL

Aveda
Aveda
Holborn Hall
193-197 High Holborn
London
WC1V 7BD

Bang & Olufsen
Bang & Olufsen UK Ltd
630 Wharfedale Road
Winnersh
Berkshire
RG41 5TP

British Airways London Eye
British Airways London Eye
Riverside Building
County Hall
Westminster Bridge Road
London
SE1 7PB

Cacharel
Cacharel Fragrances- Prestige &
Collections, L'Oréal
255 Hammersmith Road
London
W6 8AZ

Cosmopolitan
The National Magazine
Company Ltd
National Magazine House
72 Broadwick Street
London
W1F 9EP

Dazed & Confused
Dazed & Confused
112-116 Old Street
London
EC1V 9BG

Denim
Denim Investment Ltd
4 Great Queen Street
London
WC2B 5DG

Diesel
Diesel Group UK
55 Argyle Street
London
WC1H 8EF

DKNY
Donna Karen International
240 w 40th Street
New York
NY 10018
USA

Ducati
Ducati UK Ltd
Avebury House
201-249 Avebury Boulevard
Milton Keynes
MK9 1AU

Gaggia
Gaggia UK Ltd
Crown House
Mile Cross Road
Halifax
West Yorkshire
HX1 4HN

**Goldsmiths College,
University of London**
Goldsmiths College,
University of London
New Cross
London
SE14 6NW

Häagen-Dazs
General Mills UK
Harmon House
George Street
Uxbridge
Middlesex
UB8 1QQ

Hello Kitty
Sanrio Inc
Unit 38
John Wilson Business Park
Chestfield
Whitstable
Kent
CT5 3QT

Home House
Home House Ltd
20 Portman Square
London
W1H 6LN

Hope & Glory
Hope & Glory Clothing Ltd
Pembroke Studios
139-141 Pembroke Road
Muswell Hill
London
N10 2JE

Jean Paul Gaultier
Kenneth Green Associates
Hill House
Monument Hill
Weybridge
Surrey
KT13 8RX

John Rocha
Three Moon Design
The Basement
14 Hume Street
Dublin 2
Ireland

Kangol
Kangol Ltd
75 Maltings Place
Sarsons Vinegar Brewery
169 Tower Bridge Road
London
SE1 3LJ

Lambretta
Lambretta Clothing Ltd
95 Manor Farm Road
Alperton
Middlesex
HA0 1BN

Manumission
Manumission Europa
C/Agapito Llobet
7-4o4a
78800
Ibiza
Spain

Mercedes-Benz
DaimlerChrysler UK Ltd
Delaware Drive
Tongwell
Milton Keynes
MK15 8BA

Moist
Moist Ltd
4 West Burrowfield
Welwyn Garden City
Hertfordshire
AL7 4TW

MTV
MTV Networks
180 Oxford Street
London
W1D 1DF

Oakley
Oakley UK Ltd
Icon House
Icknield Way
Letchworth
Hertfordshire
SG6 1GD

Olympus
Olympus Optical Co (UK) Ltd
2-8 Honduras Street
London
EC1Y 0TX

Opium
Lafayette Restaurants Ltd
1a Dean Street
London
W1D 3RB

Po Na Na
Po Na Na Group Plc
200 Fulham Road
London
SW10 9PN

Red Stripe
Charles Wells Ltd
The Eagle Brewery
Havelock Street
Bedford
MK40 4LU

Scalextric
Hornby Hobbies Ltd
Westwood
Margate
Kent
CT9 4JX

Selfridges & Co
Selfridges
400 Oxford Street
London
W1A 1AB

South Park
The Licensing Company Ltd
Suite 2
Cumberland House
1 Kensington Road
London
W8 5NX

Star Wars
Lucas Films Ltd
5858 Lucas Valley Road
Nicadio CA 94946
USA

TAG Heuer
TAG Heuer UK
35 Brook Street
London
W1K 4HQ

Tate
Tate
Millbank
London
SW1P 4RG

The Healing Garden
Coty UK Ltd
St George's House
5 St George's Road
Wimbledon
London
SW19 4DR

The Simpsons
20th Century Fox
31-32 Soho Square
London
W1D 3AP

Time Out
Time Out Group Ltd
Universal House
251 Tottenham Court Road
London
W1T 7AB

Tommy Hilfiger
Tommy Hilfiger
European Headquarters
102 Rokin
1012 KS Amsterdam
The Netherlands

Topshop
Topshop
Colegrave House
70 Berners Street
London
W1P 3AE

Virgin Atlantic
Virgin Atlantic Airways
The Office
Crawley Business Quarter
Manor Royal
Crawley
West Sussex
RH10 9NU

Vitra
Vitra
30 Clerkenwell Road
London
EC1M 5PG

Vivienne Westwood
Vivienne Westwood
Westwood Studios
9-15 Elcho Street
London
SW11 4AU

Volkswagen Beetle
Volkswagen UK
Yeomans Drive
Blakelands
Milton Keynes
MK14 5AN

Wagamama
Wagamama Ltd
23-25 Eastcastle Street
London
W1W 8DF

Xbox
Microsoft Ltd
Thames Valley Park
Reading
Berkshire
RG6 1WG

YO! Sushi
YO! Land
95 Farringdon Road
London
EC1R 3BY